Contents

Acknowledgements

This book is an amalgam of the experiences and expertise of many women and men whose generosity with their time, thoughts and often passionate responses to my question, make up the fabric of the text. I would like to thank each one of them for taking time out of their busy schedules as parents, professionals and entrepreneurs.

Alice Bartram, Alison Grundy, Andrew Everingham, Andrew Illingworth, Angela Wong, Anna Fitzgerald, Anna Guthrie, Anne Manolas, Anne Wilkie, Brenda Minto, Caroline Macdonald, Carolyn Macadam, Catherine Lumby, Catherine Percy, Christina Hill, Christine Hemphill, Claire Hanley, Claire Johnson, Claudia Keech, Felicity Coonan, Felicity Howell, Frances, Hania Radvan, Hilary Lauder, Inge Loudon, Ivanka Belic, Jacqui Marson, Jane Sinclair, Jason Dwyer, Jenny Grant, Jeremy Halfhide, Jim Bright, Jo Dwyer, John Haviland, Judith Draper, Julia Morrissy, Julie Ritchie, Kat Callo, Kate Murphy, Kathryn McClelland, Leanne Jarrett, Leila Dean, Linda Chandler, Lisa Dukes, Lisa Hudson, Lisa Schwillie, Liz Savva, Louise Leadbetter, Lyn Cobley, Lynette Swift, Lynne Spender, Maria Czarra, Mary-Anne Stewart, Maryanne Perry, Maryouri Casas, Melinda Cilento, Melinda Pile, Melissa Halfhide, Merewyn Stivins, Michelle Brown, Michelle Sloan, Mirian Cannell, Pamela Earl, Pat Healey, Peta Lyon, Rebecca Harper, Ric Curnow, Roni Jay, Sandy Parsonson, Sasha Fidra, Seana Smith, Shevaun Haviland, Silvana Giles, Sue Lowe, Tracy Everingham, Vanessa Green, Vicki Sheehan, Victoria Hyndman, Wendy Richmond, Willa Addis.

The expert advice in this book is derived from interviews with a range of professionals, working in key recruitment roles and in the professions. The organizations that have shared their wisdom

Let Go of My Leg!

How to get the working life you want after having children

Kirsten Lees

PEARSON
Prentice Hall
BUSINESS

An imprint of Pearson Education

Harlow, England ● London ● New York ● Toronto ● Sydney ● Tokyo ● Singapore ●
Hong Kong ● Cape Town ● New Delhi ● Madrid ● Paris ● Amsterdam ● Munich ● Milan

Pearson Education Limited

Edinburgh Gate
Harlow CM20 2JE
Tel: +44 (0)1279 623623
Fax: +44 (0)1279 431059
Website: www.pearsoned.co.uk

First published in Great Britain in 2006

ISBN-13: 978-0-273-70657-1
ISBN-10: 0-273-70657-8

British Library Cataloguing-in-Publication Data
A catalogue record for this book is available from the British Library

Library of Congress Cataloging-in-Publication Data
Lees, Kirsten.
　Let go of my leg! : how to get the working life you want after having
　children / Kirsten Lees.
　　p. cm.
　ISBN-13: 978-0-273-70657-1 (alk. paper)
　ISBN-10: 0-273-70657-8 (alk. paper)
　　1. Mothers--Employment. 2. Career development. I. Title.

　HD6055.L38 2006
　650.14085'2--dc22　　　　　　　　　　　　　　　　　　　　2006046587

Designed by Sue Lamble
Cartoons by Bill Piggins

Typeset in 9/13pt Iowan by 3
Printed and bound by Bell & Bain Limited, Glasgow

The publisher's policy is to use paper manufactured from sustainable
forests.

include Swiftwork Consulting, TMP/Hudson Worldwide, Michael Page International, Heidrick & Steggles, Chandler Macleod, Challenge Consulting, Egon Zehnder International, Bradford & Peterborough Building Society, Ikea, seek.com, Monster.co.uk, Country Road Australia, Citigroup, and Telstra.

For assistance with research I would like to thank Bill Lees, Caroline Lees, John Haviland, Mary-Anne Stewart, Silvana Giles, Tracy Everingham and Vicki Nuttall.

On a personal note, I would like to thank Dr Dale Spender for providing a room with a view and no interruptions to work and for reading and commenting on the work throughout. Personal thanks, as ever, go to the women of my family: Helene Lees, Mary Anne Stewart, Caroline Macdonald, and Melissa Halfhide – whose creative and energetic lives reflect their own achievements in finding balance in their professional aspirations and their family values. And to Bill Lees, David Lees and Chris Lees whose chosen ways of dealing with so many of the same issues from the man's perspective have given me greater insights as well as suggested some resourceful and inspired solutions.

My biggest debt is, of course, to my husband Mark Woodward whose ongoing love, support and encouragement made the project – and so much else – possible, and with whom I am fortunate enough to share the great and constant learning experience that is being a parent.

Finally, gorgeous children, Emma, Chloe and Finn: you are an inspiration to us both: here's to your long, happy, creative and balanced lives.

Introduction

You've had your baby (or babies) and you've taken some time off work to set them on the path to some kind of reasonably balanced life, and now it's time to start earning again.

So what do you do?

Well, if you are a teacher or a doctor or an airline pilot, you go back to teaching, doctoring or flying planes – don't you? You just take up where you left off. Maybe your job is still open to you and you need to decide whether you still want it. Or maybe it has been a while and you feel you'll have to start from scratch. Either way, you're the same person with the same skills and qualifications as the woman who downed tools and took up play dough – even if it was months or even years ago.

Or is it that straightforward? Has what you want from the working world, and how you see yourself fitting into it, changed? Or has the working world changed while you've been busy nurturing your offspring? Very probably 'yes' – on both counts. And it'll take some careful juggling – or maybe a massive upheaval – before you can find a way to slot yourself back into its machinery and start making it work for you again.

You're not without ideas, of course. Working from home, job sharing, term-time only contracts are features of a brave new world of flexible employment you have heard so much about. But what's the reality? Are companies truly seeking out new, flexible employees? Has what we *know* really begun to count, or is it still whether we know what we know during traditional office hours that matters?

And how do you meet a job-share partner? Through the personal pages? Are two people doing one job as good as one person doing one job? It sounds better, but can you sell it to an employer?

Who has embraced these new ways of working and how have they made them work? What other options are out there for flexible work? How do you work out which one will best suit your family – and make a case for it that will make an employer sit up and listen?

Setting out on your own has a lot of appeal too – being your own boss, having your own structure, having your own deadlines. It has to be easier to work around a family to achieve your career goals. If you are going to step back on to the career ladder, why not take control of the ladder and climb it at your own pace? But how do you know if working for yourself will work for you – and who can help you get it right?

Maybe leaping straight back into the workforce is a little daunting. What about a bit more study to update old skills, develop new ones or just to get the fragmented brain stirring again? A lot of women opt for courses as a stepping stone on the path back into paid work: from a two-day computer literacy course to a full-on PhD. Updating skills, regaining confidence or just putting off the inevitable? What are the courses that help bridge the gap between playgroup and pay cheque?

However you choose to make your move, getting out of the kitchen and on to the commuter train can be daunting. And yes, uncertainty and shaky confidence and a measure of parental guilt can complicate and confuse you as you seek to make the right choices. How do you look after yourself and your family in this time of transition?

But remember, just as it can be daunting, the transition back to work is a time of opportunity and new possibilities. This may be the time to rethink career choices that you may have made (or were made for you) in your teenage years. Maybe you decide to recommit to those choices and can do so now with a mature per-spective and renewed vigour. Maybe you opt to change direction altogether.

You may have another 30 years or more of your working life ahead of you. The decisions you make over the next few months will have a great influence on how those years shape up. Think carefully. Who are you, and what do you want? What is the best way to get there?

Let Go of My Leg! is packed with insights and advice from women who have taken up the challenge and reinvigorated their careers after taking time out to be with their children – as well as from recruiters and employers who are working out how to make the most of the new, flexible workers who are being employed in greater and greater numbers.

Whatever your fears, hopes and dreams, this book will help you think through your options and design a working life that works for you.

Section 1

Getting back out there

What do I want from work?

You are thinking of going back to work. But this time you'll be a working mother. So, what has changed? And what's the same? What is it that you want? And how are you going to get your little darling to let go of your leg long enough to allow you to get out of the door?

Some of you will be preparing to go back to work after maternity leave and are thinking about how to negotiate your work and home lives to get the best out of both. Some of you may have taken a longer break and are considering how to get your skills back up to scratch before finding a job. Some of you will be happy with part-time work during school hours that helps to pay the bills, while others of you may want to launch a new career, go freelance or start your own business – or simply throw yourself into the path of opportunity and see what hits you.

Whatever your situation, the chances are you'll be looking for a job that pays, gives you some job satisfaction and leaves you enough time to spend with your family.

How do you know when it's the right time to go back?

The first step to making your transition back to work as smooth as possible is knowing the right time to start working again.

This is different for all of us. I knew it was the right time for me when that fluffy pink haze scented with talcum powder and baby oil that descended and enveloped me when each of my two daughters was born began to get a little thick. True, they were more beautiful and more absorbing (to me at least) by the day – but it was time to open some windows and let in some air.

There were other clues too, mostly in red on monthly bank statements. I got the hint. Mothering can be a great job but it doesn't pay the mortgage.

And children don't come cheap. Your child is going to cost you somewhere between £140,000 and £170,000 by the time he or she turns 21. You'll spend £50,000 of that in the first five years. How many families can afford to take on that kind of added weekly expense and drop one income for too long? Add to that the cost of your lost or reduced wages as you take time out to look after the little darling, and the £100 a week Statutory Maternity Pay is clearly put into perspective. Throw in lost pension fund contributions, national insurance payments and other entitlements and you wonder why women have children at all, let alone stop work to look after them. In fact, women have been wondering just that – and leaving children later, having fewer or choosing not to have any at all.

Luckily for the human race, women are not exclusively economically rational beings. For many of us it is still a case of 'have children first, work out how we are going to afford them later'. And 'later' does come, and that is often what speeds us back out to work, or at the very least, to sit at home pondering anxiously how on earth we are going to get a job.

- Need some stimulation and some social interaction, but money is not important at this point? What about volunteering? See Chapter 7.
- Have a great business idea and want to see if you can make it work? See Chapter 6.
- Want to keep your foot on the career ladder, and keep earning decent money – but not happy to go back to the nine-to-five? See Chapter 2.
- Trying to come up with some creative ideas on how to earn some extra cash while the baby is asleep or your children are at school – but not ready to get a job yet? See Chapter 7.

But going back to work isn't just about the money. Three-quarters of British women who work full time say they would continue working whether or not they needed the money. We enjoy working. We are good at it. We are educated and trained to work. And, as workers, we make an indispensable contribution to Britain's economic growth and social fabric.

But this is about our health and well-being too:

Real life

Having children and staying at home, there are lots of things to rob you of confidence. Lots of things happen that you have no control over – just pregnancy in itself, or breastfeeding. It is easy to sink into a black hole – a black hole of unimportant, unproductive social worth. When you get to work it is all so reasonable and so considerate. You become confident because people compliment you – you get affirmation. There are so many people around that want to tell you good things – about your work, about how you look, everything. People treat you with a lot more respect. You feel free, a fabulous freedom. You escape – everything is controllable and expectations are reasonable, so they are easy to meet. And you have entitlements, like lunch hours and how many children you are responsible for.

Sandy, relief teacher, three children

Working can be good for us. A woman's ability to earn an adequate income can be directly related to improvements in her mental and physical health. A good job that gives you a feeling of autonomy, of control over your environment and a sense of achievement can build your confidence and improve your self-esteem. You get tangible feedback at work that you don't necessarily get as a mother – like a salary. There may be pay increases or bonuses to tell you that you are doing a great job, and that you are valued. And the fact that you are sharing the household income increases your bargaining power when it comes to dividing up the housework.

The higher a woman's income, the less housework she does. According to a 2001 survey, for every £10,000 increase in her annual pay cheque, the time a woman spends doing housework drops by two hours a week.

Good and bad reasons for going back to work

Here are some good reasons for going back to work (in no particular order):

- You want to.
- You enjoy working.
- You need the money.
- You want to contribute to and be valued by society.
- You miss the company of colleagues.
- You feel ready for new challenges.
- You've got a good career idea that you want to try out.
- You want to update your skills – or learn new ones.
- You want time off from the housework.
- You need an excuse to get out of your pyjamas.
- Your self-esteem could do with the boost that you get from earning your own money, getting feedback for doing a great job and the company and respect of colleagues.
- Your children are at school all day and you have tidied the house, filled the freezer with home-made soup, rearranged the furniture (four times), found all the missing socks and colour-coded and ordered by size everything in your food cupboard. In fact, it looks so good, you find yourself rearranging the shelves in the local supermarket.

Here are some not very good reasons for going back to work:

- Pressure from your mother/sister-in-law/next-door neighbour or anybody else who feels they know what is right for you – unless you happen to agree with them.
- Everyone else seems to be.
- Pressure from your employer to return before you are ready.
- Fear that you will be left on the career shelf and that, if you don't get back now, you will be doomed to unsatisfying, low-paid work when you do decide to return. Our working lives are long – and likely to get longer. We should expect to have two, three or more careers during the course of them. If you think you need extra time now to be with your family and you can afford it then take it. The working world isn't going anywhere.

Old job or new career?

Two-thirds of us go back to work within 11 months of having a baby. And with paid maternity leave, and employers required to keep our jobs open for up to a year, most of us are going back to the job we had before we left to have our children. It makes good sense all round. You know them, they know you. You both know what to expect and frankly your life has undergone quite enough change with the new baby. You may think that the last thing you need right now is the hassle of looking for a new job, followed by the challenge of learning the ropes of a new role in a new organization. Even if you don't have a position waiting for you, looking for work doing what you have always done rather than exploring new horizons can be very appealing.

Many would agree that there is a lot of sense in the 'steady as she goes' approach when it comes to your career just after you've had a baby, with a return to the work you know – if necessary negotiating the flexibility you need. (See Chapter 2 for some ideas on this.) Tenure and track record with your employer are valuable assets, and it takes time to establish them with a new firm.

There is also the employer to consider. If you have told your company to expect you back and to keep your seat warm, you will want to manage any change in your plans with integrity. If nothing else, you'll eventually need a reference from them. You may also want to bear in mind your ongoing family plans – if you are planning a second child soon, changing jobs immediately after your first is probably unwise. It may leave you short on maternity benefits and entitlements.

Nonetheless, you cannot possibly predict how you are going to feel about your working life after your baby is born, until the time comes. Any commitment you make beforehand is made to the best of your knowledge and understanding at the time you make it. Circumstances change. And while you are bound to treat your employer and your colleagues with the respect that you would expect from them, you may decide that going back to the same job is not the right option for you.

Before you make your decision either way, it is worth examining your priorities, exploring the options that are open to you and making sure you understand the basis for whatever decision you do make. When you are up to your neck in work/family challenges it will be reassuring to know why you have made the choices that have brought you to this point.

It may be that any changes that you decide on are not to be acted on immediately but are plans for the longer term. Mapping out a path that you can follow at the right time can give you a sense of career direction and purpose, even if your immediate circumstances mean that you are happy to tread water in your career for a period.

Going back to your old job – the pros

- Your tenure and track record may make it easier to negotiate flexible terms (see Chapter 2).
- The familiarity of old faces and a familiar environment can be reassuring when you have just had the upheaval of a baby.
- An agreed 'back to work' date ensures you don't put your return off indefinitely, which can be so tempting when you have to start your job search from scratch.
- If you are going for a second child in the near future, you may not have time to qualify for maximum maternity benefits if you start a new job now.
- Even if you decide to change longer term, going back will help you decide whether you really want to change.

Real life

When I returned to work after my first child, the one thing I did that made a real difference was to promise myself that however difficult I found it, I would not do anything dramatic (resign, look for another job, give up completely, etc.) until I had been back at least six months. Despite lots of private tears (mostly to do with being away from my baby), forcing myself to stay the course for those initial six months made a real difference because six months in, I could begin to see that I could make it work. (And also, by this point, the post pregnancy hormones had finally begun to subside and I felt that any decisions I made were completely rational.)

Anne, three children

Going back to your old job – the cons

- Your old working life may no longer reflect your priorities.
- If you have taken more than a year out to look after your children you may not have a job waiting for you.
- The nature of your work simply may not accommodate being a parent.

Real life

Before we started our family I was a journalist, and owned a production company that specialized in remote and hostile areas. I spent my late twenties traipsing around war zones. When I had Tom I really felt I couldn't mix children and that job. I had to rethink.

Jacqui, psychologist and broadcaster, two children

Is it hard to get back to work?

Yes, it can be hard getting back to work after taking time out for family reasons. In fact, women with young children find it harder than any other single group to find work, according to a government commissioned report. And if it is not just any job you are after but a meaningful role with real career progression that takes into account your experience and qualifications, you may well have to tackle barriers that reflect some employers' ignorant assumption that the 'mummy track' is the only suitable career strategy.

But the barriers aren't all external. Many of us returning to work simply don't know how to work the system to get more of what we want – what we *need* – out of our working lives. It's not a greedy grab to *have it all*. Society needs women to have and nurture children, to share the care for elderly relatives, as well as to be economically active. It has educated us at considerable expense, given us experience and insights and qualities that are crucial to the economic success, cultural development and healthy evolution of our society. Society hasn't quite worked out yet how to make the most of this pool of incredible talent, and many women are stumped by the mechanics of getting back to work and reinvigorating a meaningful, rewarding career.

I certainly had a rude shock when it was my turn to look for a job after three years at home with the children. I was upbeat about my prospects. But after four weeks of applying for jobs, I hadn't had anything back from anyone – nor had I been put before an employer by any of the job agencies that I had contacted. I began to wonder. When four weeks turned into four months and the only replies to my applications were 'thanks, but no thanks', my working woman's ego was beginning to shrivel.

I began to mutter and mumble my way through the household chores. What had I done to upset the God of Getting a Great Job and Finding Work/Life Balance? Was it my CV? Or my interview suit? Or was it bad karma?

As a smarty-pants, high-achieving twenty-something, who didn't know what a child was, let alone which drawer you kept it in when you went to work each morning, I had had the opportunity to review quite a few CVs and offer people work. Maybe, unconsciously, I had been a little dismissive of anyone – any woman particularly – who was looking for work in their late thirties, or early forties, after taking time out to have children. 'Would be completely out of date, have no work ethic and probably put their children's health and happiness before my deadlines. Dreadful!'

I made a few testy calls to bemused job agencies and employment consultants demanding to know why, after all these months of looking, I wasn't CEO of something interesting, or hadn't at least landed a lucrative part-time consultancy somewhere lovely – with gorgeous clients and a great view.

Was I the only woman who found it difficult to get back into paid work after time out with her children? Or did everyone else just work through, taking the weekend off to give birth, and then go straight back to the office when all the messy bits were over? It was time for some research.

I am relieved to say that it wasn't just me. Women who stop work for a few years to concentrate on having children *do* find it difficult to get back to work. But according to the employment agencies, this is not because there are big blokes guarding the entrances to workplaces around the western world, carrying banners that read 'STOP! WRONG WAY. WOMEN WITH CAREER GAPS TURN BACK NOW'. It is because we women with career gaps have convinced ourselves that there just might be.

Of course, it is not all in the mind. There are very real barriers that are stopping women stepping back into the workforce and realizing their potential as contributors and as earners. Some of those barriers we certainly create for ourselves. They are about expectations, fear and not knowing how to prepare and present ourselves to our full advantage. Others are less in our control. They are about harsh business realities: a good employer will always pick the best person for the job. If your experience is out of date, you are in a weak position next to someone with the same qualifications but more recent experience. It is as simple as that. And then there *is* prejudice. No matter what you hear about family friendly policies, work/life balance and diversity management, few corporate cultures have truly shaken off their shackles and embraced the notion that long hours don't automatically equate to effective work, or the perception that women with children will not be as focused, as competitive or as high achieving.

Getting back to work after children is *not* straightforward – and it is an enormously important transition. It will impact on your health and well-being, as well as on the health and well-being of your family. Managed properly, it can be the first step back to a fulfilling career – either in your old industry or in a completely new direction. No pressure, but it pays to give it some thought and to get it right.

My own approach was clearly naive. I launched into my job search on that January morning as though I was the same woman, with the same goals and ambitions, the same criteria for success, operating in the same business environment as the day I left my last job to go on maternity leave. I think I even wore the same suit. (On second thoughts, after two babies, it's unlikely I would have got into it.)

But in the intervening three years, everything had changed. In a business context the company I worked for no longer existed, and colleagues were scattered in different companies and different industries. On a personal level I had of course profoundly adjusted my frame of reference. My world had shrunk. Playgroup, the park and the local pool formed three points of the triangle that bounded my daily routine with the girls. I no longer read the

Financial Times every day (I couldn't believe I ever had) and *The Economist* lay wrapped and unread in piles in the corner.

I was a different person and the world had moved on. But some things were still the same. What I wanted from my working life hadn't changed: to have my brain stretched, my ego stroked and to be paid appropriately for my contribution. If anything, time at home meant I needed all three more than ever. This meant a challenging job that allowed me to continue to learn and develop and reap the rewards of responsibility and autonomy that go with a senior role. But I also knew that I was no longer prepared to work 70 hours a week to get it.

No wonder I couldn't find a job. I wanted it all: professional rewards without professional commitment. Try putting that into a covering letter with your CV. I can hear them, as they toss my application aside: 'Well she can take a hike.'

I was still thinking about a vague, nameless 'job' and what I wanted to get out of it, but I hadn't given much thought at all to what I wanted to 'be' or how I wanted to spend my working hours. I hadn't even narrowed it down to one or two industries that interested me. Off the top of my head, I think that I applied for jobs in at least five different industries: financial services, education, media, management consulting and telecommunications. And the jobs that I was applying for were just as varied.

I worked hard on each application, trying to make each job sound like the Holy Grail of my career to date. But do you think I sounded convincing, especially when up against candidates who really did want to be whatever the particular job offered, and had guided their careers and their education and training accordingly? It was convenient to blame the fact that I had been at home with the children, but that was only part of the problem.

Finally, I had committed the job seekers' cardinal sin. Brushing aside the evidence and the advice, ignoring the wisdom and the warnings, shutting my mind even to the counsel I had so liberally handed out in the old days when I had a career and others came to me for advice – I had looked for a job in the classifieds. In fact I had based my whole job search on the small ads in the papers and online job search databases. The experts tell us that 80 per cent of jobs aren't advertised and of those that are, most are likely to be either highly specialized so that recruiters need to cast their nets wide to get the right person, or commodity jobs with high turnover, so a constant stream of candidates is required.

> A career gap of four or five years starts to get hard – but even then, if you plug away at it, you will eventually find someone to give you a break. It's harder in your head. But in fact everything comes back very quickly. Within a month you'll feel like you've never left.
>
> Anne Wilkie, Recruitment Professional, Michael Page International

Understanding the opportunity

You can be so worried about getting a job – *any* job – that you forget that things have changed, that *you* have changed and that you may never get such a great chance to reassess your circumstances and recreate your working life again. In fact, stepping away from work for a period while you have children may be just the shot in the arm your career needed.

Think about it. Having children gives women a legitimate reason to stop – even for just six months – change pace and consider our working lives from a new perspective; to look at what we have been doing from the outside and do a reality check on how closely it fits to what we want to do or who we want to be.

Men don't have this opportunity, not in the same way. 'Househusband' or 'stay-at-home dad' are still considered by many to be a thin disguise for 'made redundant and looking for work'. Unless a career break is forced upon them – and it's usually in less than pleasant circumstances – it is easy for men to be stuck on a career track they chose or fell into at 17.

Don't get me wrong. This doesn't make it acceptable for them to hog the high salaries, the promotion opportunities and the board positions. But there is a price, and it's a price that women are choosing more and more not to pay. Yes, we have been kept in middle management and out of the boardrooms – but how much do we care? Less than we did – and not always enough to sacrifice some of the things that we value more.

Women need to be in decision making roles in government, business and society. We need job satisfaction, equal pay and access to opportunities. We don't need 18-hour working days, executive burnout or to forget how to spend time with our families. One of the fastest growing sectors in human resource consulting is executive coaching – teaching senior executives the life skills they never learnt or which they forgot on the way up the career ladder.

To make the most of the opportunity that a break in your career offers, you should take some time to work out what it is you want to do. Play around with the possibilities of your potential. Invest some time, thought and imagination into coming up with your plan, then be ready to execute it with confidence.

> You read about CEOs as successful and confident and they're not. They're insecure, they have this constant sense of, 'success should feel better than this.' They don't want to show any sign of weakness; they have no friends other than work; they have no relationship with their spouse; their kids don't care about them; they have no hobbies. They lead very insular, single-dimension lives and they don't have the courage to admit it.
>
> Daniel Petre, former Microsoft executive and author of *Father Time* (Jane Curry Publishing, 2005)

Working out what you want to do

> **To work out what you want to do:**
> - Give yourself time and space to think.
> - Play with the possibilities of your potential.
> - Have the confidence to listen to yourself.
> - Surround yourself with people who believe in you and who will support you.

Before you start your job hunt, it is important to know exactly what kind of job you will be looking for. If you can be clear, people will know how to help you. If you are unclear, people will find it more difficult – they won't understand what you need, and if no one knows where to place you, your approaches to agencies and employers risk falling between the gaps. Now that so much job hunting is web based and database driven, this is even more true. As Jeff Taylor from Monster.com put it in *The Economist* (25 March, 2004):

The old saying among human-resources folk was that 'you kiss a lot of frogs before you find your prince' [...] On the internet, you kiss fewer, but only those frogs who really know what they want will find themselves on the end of their princess's puckered lips.

Listen to yourself

Most of us have a secret dream or an unscratched career itch. But not all of us have the courage to be honest about it, and it remains just that – a hidden talent, or a buried ambition, even an unrealized genius. But it is only by recognizing and acknowledging our ambitions that we can hope to realize them. The first step is to listen to yourself – you know, the little voice at the back of your mind that is so easily drowned out by everything else that is going on around you?

What are you good at? What do you enjoy? What do you do that people praise you for, or keep asking you to do or to help them with? Take time to think about past jobs and about non-work activities that you have been involved in, sports you play or committees you are on. What gives you satisfaction? What have you done that you are proud of?

Brainstorm your options. What jobs, businesses or industries might fit with the picture that is emerging? Write down any ideas that occur to you. Give your imagination some leeway. Don't stint or be shy or overly modest about what you think you are capable of.

And be careful not to restrict yourself with your pre-children assumptions about your career. Take the opportunity of the break in your career – not to mention the life changing, paradigm shattering, expectation exploding experience of having a child or two – to re-evaluate. Many women return to satisfying and rewarding careers in the industries they worked in before they had children, but many women take the opportunity – by design or by default – to reinvent their working lives. There are the high profile examples. No one can deny the benefit of J K Rowling's post-children career shift, from teacher to best-selling children's author. But we all know others. Among my own friends and neighbours I know an environmental scientist who has become a teacher, a teacher who has become a lawyer, a psychologist who has retrained to counsel school children. I know an estate agent who has become an artist, a public relations consultant who has moved into retail and a journalist who studied psychology and has become an agony aunt. All in their thirties or forties, all as a second career after children.

When you have at least 25 career options on your list (it may sound a lot, but by putting a lot down you will force yourself to think beyond the four or five obvious ones that you always go back to), start to cull. First get rid of the ideas that hold the least appeal. Then try ranking the remaining ideas according to preference. As you rank each job, think about why you like it more or less than the others. Use your ranking to help you cut the list further until you have a manageable handful of jobs, businesses or industries that really interest you.

Next go public. Try out your ideas on friends and family. How do they respond? (If they fall about laughing, it may not be the career idea you want to change but your so-called friends, though it is not so easy to ditch your family.) Bouncing your ideas around with other people will help to refine them. Listen to what others have to say, but most importantly listen to yourself as you describe your emerging ambitions. Can you get excited about yourself in the new incarnation that you are considering? Can you believe in your own ability to achieve it?

Do some research into the jobs that remain on your list. What do they entail? What further training or study might you need? What opportunities might there be for work in this field? What is the pay like? What other rewards might this kind of work offer? As the information fleshes out your understanding of the different options you have on your list, you will lose interest in some and be more attracted to others.

> ### Start working out what you would like to do:
>
> 1 Brainstorm at least 25 career options.
> 2 Cull the list, losing those that hold the least appeal.
> 3 Rank the remaining options in order of preference.
> 4 Use your rankings to cull further until you have a list of four or five jobs.
> 5 Go public – test your ideas with friends and family.
> 6 Research the jobs on your list and use the information you gather to further refine your thoughts.

Claire had a successful career as an accountant and auditor. It took two children and some time out to give her the confidence to go for what she had always wanted to do:

I have always been passionate about the environment, and at school I imagined myself studying something like environmental geography then working in the not-for-profit sector. My dad was against it. 'Get yourself a real job,' he kept saying. So when I left school and was offered a job with Arthur Andersen at the same time as a university place to study geography, I took the job with Andersens and became an accountant. At that age I didn't know. I didn't have the confidence to stand up and say this is what I really want to do.

I left Andersens as soon as I was qualified, and went to work at a small accounting practice in Central London. I was good at it and I ended up running the practice. But I knew that this wasn't what I really wanted and kept looking for something else. Finally I was thrilled to be offered the opportunity to go to Africa with Save the Children – then I found out I was pregnant, which meant I couldn't go.

Claire continued to earn her living as an auditor, using her experience and her reputation to buy some flexibility. After her second child was born, she took a look at her options and decided it was time finally to do what she had always wanted. She enrolled in a Masters in Environmental Management. She has done a two-year degree slowly over three years, studying mostly in the evening and doing block units during the holidays:

Real life

This time around I know what I want, and I am really going to go for it. The environmental industry is small – and it is very competitive. I am finding it hard even to get volunteer work with the kind of NGOs [non-governmental organizations] that interest me. I take contract work as an accountant to keep money coming in, but I won't be tempted to go back into it full time. I've let it go before. I am going back to work to realize my dream. I won't let it go again.

Claire, accountant and environmental manager, two children

Take a reality check

As you start narrowing down your options you should begin to consider what you want out of your working life – the tangible, day to day mundanities that can make your life easier and more manageable, like finding a job within commuting distance or a work environment in which you feel comfortable.

How important are pay, conditions, schedule, promotion prospects, responsibility and recognition? Does flexibility need to be part of the package – as an upfront *must have* or a *will negotiate later?* Are the hours each day or the days each week that you are available to work limited, and will that change over time? Does the distance you can travel from home each day restrict where you can take a job? Do you want to work for yourself, or do you see yourself as part of a team?

Is it a full-time or part-time role as Academy Award winning film director that you would consider? Or would you compromise with a job share? Will you need to leave the set early each day to pick up the children? Or could they be flown out to the location?

See Table 1.1 for a whole series of practical questions that will help you clarify your thinking and transform your dream into a realizable career goal.

Thinking through the practical aspects of your working life will help you further narrow down your options and clarify what kind of industry or job might suit you best. Don't worry that being too specific about what you want early on may limit potential opportunities. They are only opportunities for you if you are

Table 1.1: What to consider when choosing your job

What kind of work environment are you looking for?

Casual or formal?

Variety or conformity?

Hectic or quiet?

Collaborative or independent?

Lots of people or few?

Indoor or outdoor?

Office based or mobile?

Team oriented or autonomous?

Open plan or private space?

What kind of activities?

Deadline driven?

Customer-facing?

Project based?

Innovative?

What do you look for in a boss?

Clear direction or freedom to make your own decisions?

A collaborative style, mentoring approach, or very directed?

What kind of reward system are you after?

Salary based, incentive scheme, or combination?

Permanent, contract, freelance, casual?

Promotion prospects?

Clear career path?

Opportunities for on-the-job training?

Recognition and status?

What sector do you see yourself in?

Small business?

Private enterprise?

Academia?

Not-for-profit/non-government organization?

Multinational?

What working conditions do you expect?

Flexible work options?

Paid overtime

Childcare facilities

Business travel opportunities

On-the-job training?

Company sponsored education and/or study leave?

Parental leave?

Where do you want to work?

Within a defined commuting time to allow school drop offs, etc.?

Only in your local area?

Near public transport?

With accessible parking?

At home some or all of the time?

able to take them up. There is little value in finding the perfect job share in North Vladivostock if your three teenagers are at high school in Derby (or is there?).

When a job does come up, you may find that you need to bend a bit. But clarity and understanding of how you want your working life to look and how it needs to fit with your other responsibilities will make it easier to focus any negotiations on what you want and need.

Get help

The answer to your career question is within you – and you either know what it is or have a pretty good idea already. You may need the confidence to articulate it, or some help to refine it, and to work out your plan to get where you want to be. There is a range of help available – from career professionals and back-to-work courses, to support networks based around industry groups and women's networking organizations, as well as the men and women you know who have faced similar dilemmas and understand what you are going through.

Careers advisers

If you are going back to your career after a reasonable break, it is very useful to sit down and piece together a picture of your working past. Some people benefit from the structure and support that a session with a careers adviser can provide.

When you enrol on a course at technical college, university or with one of the many private colleges, you will often have access to some sort of career guidance service. If you don't, you may decide to go to one of the many career advisers who can be found in the *Yellow Pages* or online, and who charge a fee for their service.

If you choose this option, take time to find someone with the right qualifications and experience with the industries that you are considering, and at the level you are hoping to enter. Get a personal referral if possible. Careers advisers offer a variety of services, from providing encouragement to orchestrating your whole job search strategy. Their charges vary but they are not generally cheap. Take advantage of the offer of a free initial consultation, to get to know the adviser and check that the services offered will meet your needs.

A careers adviser may also use some of the extensive profiling tools on the market that are designed to gauge your personality, inclinations, strengths and weaknesses, aptitudes and abilities. These are big business and there is a multitude of tests, tools and exercises that will get you thinking about where your skills lie and what you enjoy: for example, writing a mini autobiography; telling seven tales of childhood achievements; listing all the awards and recognition you have received professionally and personally from Brownie badges to bursaries. There are worksheets, questionnaires, quizzes and tests that will profile your personality, define your type, measure your aptitude and give you your own personal spot on someone's quadrant. If you are interested in trying out some of these tests, there are some available online. Eventually, via a complex and thoroughly scientific process, your secret path to career success will be revealed.

Be realistic about what you can expect. The answer to the question, 'What do I really want to do?' isn't out there in someone else's database. The tests and other tools may help you to identify it and give you the words to articulate it, and a career counsellor may help you map out your path to achieving it – but the answer is within you.

My own experience with a careers adviser – before I left school admittedly – showed that I had the personality profile, skills and attributes for a career in creating railway timetables. That is honestly what I was told. How they possibly uncovered that nugget from a shy teenager with a passion for volcanoes and tectonic plates and an interest in European languages is a mystery to me, but I do know that I filled out a lot of forms first.

In many cases, people who give the best advice are those who have faced similar dilemmas and choices. Talking to as many women as possible about what they do and what their work involves may prove to be as valuable as a session with a careers adviser.

Courses for women returning after a career break

If you have been out of the workforce for a while and are feeling daunted by the prospect of getting your CV together and getting

▶ Psychometric and aptitude tests

If you would like to sample some psychometric and aptitude tests, the following websites have free samples:

www.peoplemaps.co.uk – take a ten-minute test and receive a brief report – a 'try before you buy' approach.

www.assessment.com – gives you an idea of the kind of questions you would expect. The report is brief.

http://www.shldirect.com/ – SHL is a major UK based test provider. Has practice tests and feedback online.

www.psychtesting.org.uk – run by the British Psychological Society, this lists a number of sites which offer free psychometric tests.

www.mypotential.net – has demo tests and reports which you can view.

http://practicetests.cubiks.com – has free numerical and verbal practice tests rather than psychometric.

http://www.bbc.co.uk/skillswise – has free numerical and verbal practice exercises to help you to improve your skills.

to grips with some of the changes in technology since you have been at home, there are courses run especially for women who fit this profile. You can find details through your local tech college or university, through private providers online or by going to your local library.

A considerable advantage of doing one of these courses is that they put you in touch with other people facing the same issues as you. It can be an enormous relief to find out that you aren't the only one who feels out of touch with work, mystified by technology and terrified of making a fool of yourself. Some courses, like Career Action for Women (run by the Centre for Continuing Education at the University of Sussex and funded by the European Social Development Fund), offer free childcare and travel expenses. Learn Direct publishes a list of courses that can be downloaded from www.learndirect.co.uk, or you can call them on freephone 0800 100 900 or access their careers advice website at www.learndirect-advice.co.uk. The Women Returners Network is a registered charity which provides information and advice for women returning to work, including information on courses. You can contact them via their website at www.women-returners.co.uk.

Industry associations run refresher courses, while trade fairs allow you to catch up with what is going on in a particular field.

Map out your path

Once you have a picture of what it is you want to do, you will need to be able to describe the steps that will lead you to your goal.

You will need to be able to answer the following questions:

- What kind of training/further study do I need?
- Is there an apprenticeship?
- How long will it take before I can expect to be fully qualified?
- What daily/weekly time commitment will I need to make?
- Will there be travel involved?
- Will I need to secure funding?
- Will I need to involve other people?
- Are there opportunities in my local area?
- Can I create the opportunities I need?

The next trick is to break down the journey, however long, into small, achievable steps.

Big steps might look like this:

1　Finish BA in Communications I started ten years ago.
2　Do volunteer work for local radio.
3　Check my network for contacts in the radio industry.
4　Get a paid job in local radio.
5　Become a shock-jock talkback radio host, with big business in my pocket and influence over leading politicians.

Or, if you are like me and need things on a more manageable scale, you might break them right down:

1   Find paperwork for that course I started at university in the mid-1990s.
2   Phone up and see if I can re-enrol.
3   Phone my local education authority and see if I can get a student loan.
4   Fill out application forms.
5   Post application forms for the course.
6   Post application forms for the loan.

And so on, tiny steps all the way to being a radio megastar, without ever taking on anything too big or too daunting.

Are you able and willing to do what you need to do to achieve your goal?

Real life

We have talked for ages about opening a cafe or a restaurant – going back into hospitality. We have looked at a few opportunities and gone into what it would take to get a good business up and running. I know that we could do something fantastic together. But when we considered the numbers and looked at the risks, we decided against it. We have three children, the eldest is about to start high school. We need to be earning right now. Putting everything into a business that would probably not turn a profit for two years would not be the right thing for us now. We know who we are, we know our bottom line, but at this point in our lives, we can't take on that kind of risk, or make those kinds of sacrifices.

Jo, stay-at-home mother, three children

It is vital to have a realistic perspective on what you are able to and prepared to do to realize your career goals. You may find that now is the wrong time to launch a new business venture, or that the five-year degree course to qualify you in your chosen field is not a time frame you are able to work with. Hosing down your bright idea with a cold shower of reality every now and then is healthy. If you find you are not able to commit to your number one career path, all is not lost. You can rethink the role, choose a different role in the same industry, change your time frame or bring other people in to help you. If all else fails, go back to your list and explore some of your other options and see if you find a better fit.

Make sure that you recognize the difference between being realistic and being fearful. It is easy to create barriers to hide behind. Fear of change can stop us exploring new possibilities and challenging how we live our lives. Yet it also stops us taking unnecessary risks and making costly mistakes. It is important to know the difference.

Be prepared to recognize when something isn't working, to stop, to rethink and give it another go – or put your hands up and admit that you're on the wrong track altogether if you have to. This is not failure. It is shifting the goal posts a little, but if every time you shift the goal posts you make it more likely that you will achieve your goal, what is wrong with that? Do it as often as you need to.

Being too old, it being too late in your career or not having the right qualifications are no longer an excuse to stay in jobs we don't enjoy or careers we don't find rewarding. There are almost half a million mature-aged students in higher education – and that doesn't count the mature students at private colleges or training organizations. Women who go back to work in their forties have another 20 years' working life ahead – or more if they choose. It is now *normal* to have two or three or even four careers. Why not make one of them something you have always wanted to do? And why not make it now?

You should now have worked out whether you want to go back to the same job or a similar job, or strike out in a new direction. In Chapter 3 we will get you started on actually finding and getting that job, if that's what you're now set on, but before that we will take a closer look at flexible working.

Flexible work

One of the first things to get your head around as you prepare your return to work is what kind of hours you plan to do. Do you want to work full time or part time? Are you interested in a job share or working from home?

Whether you are going back to your old job and plan to renegotiate your hours or you are searching for a new job with flexible work in mind, you need to know what it means for you and your employer.

It is also worth keeping flexible work negotiations in mind when you are looking for a new job but seem to find the kind of work you want advertised only as full-time roles. It may be that the employer has not thought about how the role can be done differently. A positive approach with a realistic and workable flexible alternative may get a good hearing. It worked for Anne when she was discussing a position with a textile design company:

I knew I had to be up front about what I could and couldn't do. I didn't want to get myself into the situation I had been in in my previous job where there was no understanding of my need for some flexibility. At the first interview I asked if I could be part time not full time and I was quite specific about the hours I could do. She agreed, and then I brought up the holidays issue. I explained that with two children at school I would need more time off during the holidays – at least to be able to drop down to two days a week. She was fine about this, perhaps because I was up front. There is nothing in writing, but the deal is that I give her plenty of notice and manage my work around the time I need off.

What is flexible work?

Flexible work is flexibility in when and where you get your job done. It can mean working at home a couple of days a week, having flexible start and finish times or structuring your working year around school term times. It can be as complex and formally structured as a permanent job-share arrangement or as simple as an unstated understanding with your boss that you will work late one day because you need time to take your child to the dentist the next.

Women have been fitting paid work in around their families ever since they have had families, but how they do it has always been a 'woman's issue' – a 'mother's problem' and usually a 'mummy track' option.

Things have changed. The many balls of the work/family juggling act have landed squarely in the lap of business – big and small – not to mention on to the pages of policy papers of the leading political parties, even making the statute books. Since April 2003 parents with children under the age of six, or disabled children under 18, have had the right to request a flexible work arrangement without penalty – and employers have to consider the request seriously.

Why does it suddenly matter to our captains of industry that you get the quality time you need with your children? And why is the government involved? If they've gone gooey about whether you are home in time to read a bedtime story a couple of times a week, you would think they'd get the trains to run on time.

Not surprisingly, it is the *work* side of the work/family balancing act that business and government are most interested in. Work – somebody has to do it. And, as 44 per cent of the workforce and 60 per cent of undergraduate students, women are doing a lot of it. Mothers or not, women are fundamental to the nation's ongoing economic viability and future growth. With the slowing birth rate and the gradual decline in numbers of people of traditional working age to support a swelling number of older, non-working Britons, each one of us has to be more productive. Government and business have worked out (*hello?*) that to make women more productive, it has to be possible for them to run their family lives while they continue to work – or when they choose to come back to work.

Key facts

- Women are 44 per cent of the working population.
- Sixty-seven per cent of women go back to work after having children.
- Fifty per cent of women with children under five work.
- Women are 60 per cent of undergraduate students.
- Women have been graduating in larger numbers than men from higher education for more than ten years.
- Women earn 82 per cent of men's hourly rate.
- Thirty per cent of all jobs are part time.
- Seventy-seven per cent of parents of children under six consider 'work/life balance' a key factor when considering a job.
- Sixty-eight per cent of parents would like access to flexitime.

At the same time, the kind of work we do and how we do it has changed. Western economies are no longer about things you can drop on your foot – it is a service economy. The old industries of mining and manufacturing relied on workers being at a particular place (at the factory or down the mine) at a given time (office hours or the start of a shift) to get the job done. In the service industries and in an information economy, what we sell is often intangible: knowledge, contacts, relationships, creativity, experience, understanding the market, spotting new opportunities, goodwill, brands and so on.

Who does the work suddenly matters more than *where* they do it or when – their knowledge, skills, creativity and connections. Companies have been making warm, fuzzy statements about the importance of their employees for decades. Now they are beginning to mean it.

For workers it is a sellers' market. And, as we negotiate our terms and conditions of employment, it is clear that money isn't the only motivator. In a Department of Trade and Industry survey, flexibility ranked higher than a pay rise for two-thirds of employees, and way higher than free gym membership. This suits companies which are looking for new ways to attract and motivate the right people. Flexible work arrangements are coming up as an answer for both sides.

What flexible work arrangements are there?

Permanent part time: Fewer hours, for pro-rata pay, holidays and leave entitlements.

Flexible time: Flexible start and finish time, usually around core hours with the ability to bank hours worked to take as leave at a later date.

Working from home/telecommuting/flexiplace: Allows employees to work from home either all or part of the time.

Job share: Dividing the workload of a full-time position between two people working part time.

Study leave: Leave taken to study for a specific course or skills, can be work related but not necessarily.

Term-time only work: Employers are contracted to work only during term time with unpaid leave during school holidays. (Pay can be averaged out over 12 monthly instalments to provide a regular income.)

Compressed working week: A full-time job in a reduced number of days – say a 38-hour week in four rather than five days.

Career breaks: Time off unpaid with the job held open.

Annualized hours: An agreed number of hours worked during the year, adjusted according to business demand.

Holiday purchase scheme: An arrangement that enables employees to buy an additional day's holiday on top of their annual entitlement.

Other work arrangements: These include parental leave, long service leave, family leave and access to childcare.

Is flexible work widely available?

Well, that depends what you mean.

If you include part-time work, and most figures do, then flexible work is very widely available and women are getting what they want. In fact, more than 40 per cent of all women who work – close on five and a half million women – work part time. The numbers of part-time jobs are increasing and the number of women asking to go part time after having children is going up too.

That is all well and good, but it's hardly the brave new world of telecommuting and job sharing, is it? More importantly, while part-time work is one significant option for women who want to continue working and keep at least half an eye on the children, does it address all the issues?

Part-time work can be as inflexible as full-time work, but just shorter hours and less pay. Does it offer flexibility to keep your foot on the career ladder, and to be available and considered for promotion, for training or other opportunities if you are interested? Is there scope to negotiate what those part-time hours are, and are they structured to reflect the business goals you are employed to achieve – or has someone simply cut your job and your pay in two without further thought?

There is no doubt that part-time work is an important option for women trying to care for children and earn themselves a living. And there can be great benefits in cutting down your hours for a period of months or even years. But although your employer has to consider your request to work part time, there is no obligation for him or her to give you back full-time hours when you are ready to work more. That sounds pretty inflexible to me. Unless it is thought through carefully, a part-time job risks being a 'mummy track' option which leaves women in lower paid jobs, with fewer savings, fewer promotion prospects and fewer opportunities should they wish to revitalize their careers when the children have learnt to fend for themselves – or their husbands have opted for a younger model, taking the retirement plan with them. (Fifty-two per cent of UK marriages now end in divorce. It is naive not to be prepared for the possibility.)

A company wishing to flaunt its family friendly credentials has to have more than the part-time option to offer parents. True flexibility should allow employees – men and women – to maintain some kind of career momentum during the intense parenting years. (I understand there are at least 18 of them.)

After part-time work, the widely available flexible work options are flexitime, job sharing, and term-time only contracts

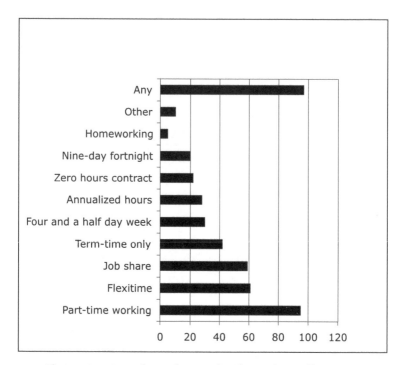

Figure 2.1: Number of organizations that offer different flexible work practices

From 'Flexible working practices', Research Report prepared for Equal Opportunities Commission and People Management, April 2005, available at http://www.eoc.org.uk/pdf/flexible_working_practices.pdf

(see Figure 2.1). Fewer than a third of organizations offer a four and a half day week, annualized hours, zero hours contract or a nine-day fortnight. Most surprisingly in these days of wireless broadband and related communications technologies, only 5 per cent of organizations surveyed offered employees the opportunity to work from home.

Are flexible work arrangements successful?

For employers

When companies are asked whether their family friendly policies work, they say 'yes' almost without exception. Most often the benefits that companies claim are difficult to measure in business terms. They include things like 'improved morale' and 'better work/life balance'. The thinking goes something like: happy staff are healthier, more loyal, less likely to be looking for another job, more likely to come back after maternity leave and less likely to take sick leave.

More work is being done to put a monetary value on these improvements. One study claims that the share price of companies in the FTSE 100 which have clear work/life balance policies outperform the share prices of other similar companies by around 5 per cent. Such statistics are difficult to prove, but if each time you recruit a manager it costs you around £7000 – not counting the knowledge lost when the old manager leaves and the time it takes a new person to come up to speed – there are real financial benefits in keeping your employees happy. A green paper, 'Work & Parents: Competitiveness and Choice', prepared for the British government quotes the cost of training lost each time the NHS loses a doctor to be £200,000 – and £34,000 for every nurse that leaves the system.

The following benefits of flexible work policies were listed by employers in a survey carried out by the Equal Opportunities Commission in 2005:

- Improved morale, 25 per cent
- Increased staff retention, 24 per cent
- Improved ability to attract and retain staff, 11 per cent
- Improved work/life balance for employees, 11 per cent
- Flexible staff numbers, 5 per cent
- Improved customer service, 5 per cent
- Reduced absenteeism, 4 per cent
- No benefits at all, 4 per cent

Where companies are still struggling to implement flexible work arrangements the challenges are often cultural, based on what people are used to, and their reluctance to change. Flexible work arrangements will continue to be mistrusted and misunderstood in any business culture that rewards long hours rather than rewarding employees on what they achieve when at work. But mostly it seems that line managers are unsure how to make flexible arrangements work, how to manage staff on flexible rosters or working from home, and how to manage a team where some members have what may appear to be favourable arrangements.

Real life

So much depends on your manager. I was fortunate with my boss as she had a child of her own. She had prior working knowledge of both my job-share partner and myself and was extremely supportive when we said we wanted to come together. But even if your manager is onside you have to work to bring your peers along with you. You are going to have to deal with 'looks' occasionally when you leave on time, or say that you aren't available for a meeting – it helps if you have been in your job for a while and have shown you are a performer but it is even more important that once you are in the job-share role you continue to demonstrate high performance.

Peta, financial services, two children

In companies where flexible working arrangements are available, they have made limited inroads into more than a few specific types of jobs and levels of seniority. People are used to seeing particular jobs done in particular ways. Companies may be reluctant to translate positions that include high exposure to customers, a lot of business travel or a considerable amount of people management into flexible arrangements – but this doesn't mean it can't be done.

There are probably 500 people in this country who dictate the work environments for everybody and if they get this right, which then manifests itself in how they behave and how they manage people, they get this incredible leveraged effect where the person on the shop floor on $35,000 with two kids would start to get a better work environment too.

Daniel Petre, former Microsoft executive and author of *Fathertime*

For workers

Since the law changed in April 2003, almost a quarter of UK employees with dependent children under six have requested the right to work flexibly. Four-fifths of these requests have been granted. And four-fifths of those who have made the switch to flexible working arrangements say they are satisfied with how things are going. Companies with the greatest range of flexible work options have the highest rates of women returning after maternity leave.

Those who have experienced a downside in the change rank the reduction in pay as the biggest negative, followed by intensified workload and deterioration in relationship with colleagues and managers. But these negative experiences seem far outweighed by the positive.

> ### How employees see the benefits of flexible work:
>
> - Time with family, 37 per cent
> - Free time, 25 per cent
> - Reduced stress, 12 per cent
>
> How employees see the negatives of flexible work:
>
> - Reduction in pay, 22 per cent
> - Other negatives: intensified workload, deterioration in relationship with colleagues and managers

There is still no evidence that a job-share arrangement or any other flexible work option is the fast track up the company ladder, but there are plenty of women who have used flexible work arrangements as a way to keep a foot on the ladder while they manage family responsibilities, ready to return to the corporate climb when and if priorities change once again and they refocus on their careers.

Vanessa, a senior manager in a London PR company, negotiated a four-day week when she returned from her first maternity leave:

I reduced my hours to four days so that I could have a whole day each week with my son. He had two days at nursery and a day with each set of his grandparents. Despite going part time I was promoted to operational board level, and was supervising staff. I am a very conscientious person and as a senior staff member I was very aware of how the business was going – what pressures and challenges it was facing. It was a tough environment – even though the company was family friendly. It is difficult to work in a demanding environment and still have plenty of time during the week with your kids.

There was never any open pressure, but I did feel a frisson of resentment – mostly from the people I supervised, who would work long hours, while I was only in the office four days a week. I knew that I had my head down a lot more than I did before I had children, but I didn't feel safe. We were facing a lot of redundancies and everyone was under particular pressure to perform.

When I had my second child, I knew that I couldn't make the kind of commitment I believed my job needed from me, and working part time wasn't going to work. I took eight months off then decided not to go back.

PR is a very demanding industry. For me, in a senior position, I felt I had to make a choice about my priorities. Part time wasn't an option for me in a senior role.

What are our rights and responsibilities with regard to flexible work arrangements?

The right to paid maternity leave

All pregnant employees are entitled to 26 weeks' paid maternity leave. If you have been with the company more than six months three months before your baby is due, you can take an additional 26 weeks unpaid.

To qualify, you need to tell your employer:

● Fifteen weeks before your expected due date (they've probably guessed something is up by now).

- When you are due.
- When you plan to start your maternity leave.

The right to paid paternity leave

Fathers are entitled to two weeks' paid paternity within two months of the baby's (or babies') birth. Remember, this is down in the statute books as leave 'to care for the baby *and support the mother'*. Milk it.

The right to return to the same job after maternity leave

Women returning to work after maternity leave (and men returning after paternity leave) have the right to return to the same job they held before they went on leave. The terms and conditions must be the same – or better – and if the rest of the team has had a pay rise during the period of leave then it must be included in the pay. If the position has become redundant, the employer must offer a suitable alternative job, with similar terms and conditions.

The right to breastfeed

Women have no legal rights for time off to breastfeed or express milk while at work. However, health and safety guidelines recommend 'time off without loss of pay or benefits and without fear of a penalty'.

The recommendations include adequate rest and meal breaks, and somewhere to take a rest where you can lie down. In France breastfeeding women are allowed two 30-minute breaks a day, while in Italy they are allowed two hour-long breaks daily. In Australia employers must provide a private room with lockable door, a power point and a small fridge. (Australians realize that it helps if you can mix a decent cocktail – or at least have a cold beer – to get your milk flowing. That's why they call it the Lucky Country!)

The right to part-time work or flexible work arrangements

All parents with children under six or disabled children under 18 have the right to request a flexible working arrangement and their employers have a duty to consider the application seriously. The reason for the request must be specifically to allow the parent to participate in childcare arrangements. It is the right to *ask* and not to be penalized for asking. The employer has no obligation to say 'yes', but does have to give it serious thought. A summary of the regulations is available online from the Department of Trade and Industry.

If you make a request and it is refused, it must be on clear business grounds. Reasons that a business might reasonably give to refuse include:

- The burden of additional costs.
- A detrimental effect on ability to meet customer demand.
- An inability to organize work among other employees.
- The inability to recruit additional employees.
- A detrimental effect on quality.
- A detrimental effect on performance.
- Insufficient work when the employee proposes to work.
- Planned structural changes.

If an employer refuses your request, the reasons must be detailed and in writing, and you have the right to appeal.

The change to the working arrangement is permanent unless agreed otherwise upfront.

Responsibilities

Like any employee, flexible workers have responsibilities to their employer. They have a responsibility to work to agreed deadlines, to work to agreed standards and to communicate regularly with managers, project teams and peers.

But even with successful flexible work arrangements, there are possible pitfalls associated with being out of the office that both the employer and the employee should work to avoid.

If you are working away from the office, or are less visible because you are working fewer or irregular hours, there is a chance that you will not be seen as part of the team. With the best will in the world on both sides, out of sight can mean out of mind, and flexible work may increase your chances of being passed over when it comes to the kind of opportunities that we take for granted around the workplace: opportunities for training, to take part in organizational development, for promotion; the chance to act in more senior roles and to find out what vacancies and other opportunities may be available around the organization.

Electronic communications make this less of an issue – the corporate intranet of most larger organizations can keep employers in touch with so much that is going on around the workplace, from the latest job vacancies to the day's menu in the canteen. Nevertheless, your employer still has a responsibility to make sure that you have the same access to training and development, promotion and knowledge of vacancies as a non-flexible worker.

But if you want to make your flexible work arrangement really successful, it is important that you share the responsibility for making sure that your absence doesn't disadvantage you. You need to work at keeping yourself visible, reminding everyone who you are, where you are and what a great job you are doing, even if they can't see you every day.

Make sure you interact regularly with your manager, but also with other people around the office. Ask questions and if you need help or advice from a colleague, ask for it. Just because you work irregular hours or from home doesn't mean you are expected to know everything. This kind of peer to peer interaction will make you part of the team more than anything else.

One of the advantages of working from home is that you don't have to attend Friday night drinks every week – but that is also one of the disadvantages. Going back to work after children is often as much about social interaction as it is about achieving career goals and making some money. Make the effort to attend some social events – it will help consolidate personal relationships and keep you up with the gossip. Treat your colleagues like your network: it needs nurturing, occasionally updating and staying in touch with. Your colleagues are a valuable source of support, information, workplace gossip, experience and advice.

Many of them will understand from personal experience the work/family juggling act you are trying to manage and encourage you in it and admire you for it.

Negotiating flexible work

Asking for a job share because you 'want more time with your toddler' or for flexitime because you 'can't get decent after school care' may seem perfectly valid, but your boss is unlikely to be impressed. Despite all the talk of the world changing and work-places becoming more family friendly, there are still deals to do, targets to meet and customers to serve. As far as your boss is concerned, as long as you are part of the business, you are part of that picture and have a responsibility to pull your weight.

So *how* you put your case matters. You need to convince your boss that what you are proposing is good for business. Remember, it is the 'right to *request*' flexible work and for the organization to give the request 'serious consideration' that have become enshrined in law. Just because you are a parent, you don't get an automatic early mark every day – unfortunately.

Think of your request to work more flexibly as a business proposition, not some kind of favour that you are asking. Take a business focused approach. Research the issue. Anticipate objections and counter them before they are raised. Prepare a detailed plan of how your new arrangement will work day to day and always emphasize the benefits to the organization.

Doing all the research, thinking through how your new flexible work arrangement is going to work and putting it in writing will make it more easily understood and agreed to. Importantly, it will also make the new way of working much easier to manage down the track. You will know what you have committed to and what expectations your boss and your colleagues will have, and it will be easier to spot any problems as they arise and deal with them straight away.

A persuasive proposal like this need not take long to prepare and you don't need a business degree to do it. The steps are simple and the information you will need to put your case is readily available.

To put together a persuasive business case for flexible work, you will need to follow these steps:

Step 1: Determine which flexible arrangement will work best
Step 2: Do your research
Step 3: Put together your action plan
Step 4: Present your proposal.

Step 1: Choose a flexible work arrangement

There are two sides to this – which flexible work arrangement will work for *you*, and which one will best suit the organization. The trick is to understand clearly what your needs are and the needs of the business, then to look for a solution that will work for both, as far as possible.

Why are you asking for flexible work?

Think carefully and in detail about what flexibility really means for you. Do you need the flexibility to do daily, predictable tasks like pick children up from school or childcare, or do you need a day or two during the week to spend with a pre-school child? Do you need flexibility for regular but more extended periods, like during the school holidays? Is your need for flexibility unpredictable – being able to stay at home to look after a sick child from time to time or take time off to go to school performances, for example?

Write a list of what you are hoping to be able to achieve once you have a more flexible schedule or no longer need to commute into the office every day. Order the list in terms of priorities. What on the list is most important to you? Is there anything you are prepared to negotiate?

Will your job suit a flexible arrangement?

There are few jobs that can't cope with a bit of flexibility – whether it is a few hours a week working from home or a more radical redesign and job share. In the digital economy, enabled as we are by the broadband internet and the communications revolution, it is less and less important when and where we do our job, but *what* we do that counts.

To find out if your job suits a more flexible arrangement, you will need to make three lists. First, write down what you do when you are at work: consider the characteristics of your job, your main duties and responsibilities, your lines of communication and your business goals. Your job description will be helpful if you have one. Alternatively, keep a diary for a few days of how you spend your working day.

Second, list the busy periods and quieter times as far as they are predictable. If the flow of activity is steady or unpredictable, note that too. Think about when the busy times fall – during the day, the week or over the whole year.

Finally, think about how your work fits in terms of what the organization is trying to achieve and the challenges it faces. Does your organization have enough work space for everyone? Is it focused on keeping costs down? Are there heavy overtime bills that are causing concern? Is there a high turnover of staff, and with it a regular drain of corporate knowledge and experience?

Half of IBM's 10,000 employees in Australia/New Zealand work from home for a minimum of four hours a week. This is a huge saving for the company. Telecommuting combined with a policy of hot-desking keeps the cost of office space and overheads down – and it retains women who take maternity leave. The return rate has risen from 74% to 94% since IBM has introduced telecommuting.

Dr Dale Spender, 'Changing lanes: finding a new career/life direction', Spokeswomen's Program Speech, given 6 May 2004, Sydney.

Step 2: Do your research

Once you have decided which flexible work arrangement you are going to propose, you need to start building your argument. You will need four or five specific, relevant facts or examples to strengthen your case and to make sure that your request for flexible work gets a reasonable hearing. Asking around the organization about other flexible workers and doing some web based research will give you what you need.

The places to go to find the information you will need are:

1 **Your company policy.** Are there any human resources policies? Work/life balance issues may not have filtered down to your manager, but that doesn't mean that the company doesn't have a perspective or set of policies. Ask your human resources department if you have one. Check the website or the company intranet. How does the company describe itself to the outside world? Family friendly? Equal opportunity employer? Do a media search to see if it has made public statements on family friendly issues. If you work for a multinational, is there a 'Global Director of Diversity' or 'VP Human Resources' that you can quote? The most persuasive argument will be the one built using the company's own words to present your case.

2 **Precedents.** Are there other people in your organization doing flexible work? Talk to them. How did they make their case? What arguments did they have to counter? Is the arrangement working? Do they have numbers to show this? Can you get testimonials from this person's peers, customers or manager?

3 **Colleagues.** Talk to colleagues, especially those with whom you interact most. Can you get them to back your initiative?

4 **Competitors.** What are competitors doing? If your business competitors are offering more flexible terms and conditions, it can be a threat to your company's ability to attract and retain top staff – worth pointing out. Tap into your network, check out their websites. Do they have persuasive family friendly policies? Are they making them work? Is there evidence?

5 **Check out your customers.** What are your customers doing in this area? Proving cultural fit with key customers is a strong business argument. Can their flexible work practices strengthen your argument?

Step 3: Put together your action plan

Your action plan is the document that you will present to your boss when you propose your flexible work arrangement. It does not need to be long or complex. In fact, the more concise and simple, the better. Once the arrangement has been approved and is in place, this document can be a useful measure of its success.

The executive summary

Start with an executive summary and make it a concise, punchy summary of what follows. The idea is, when you slide your proposal across the desk to your boss, a quick scan of your summary will let them know what you are asking for and why you should get a favourable hearing (apart from the fact that the law says you must). The detail comes later.

A half-page to a page will be enough. You should include what you are proposing, how the company will benefit and two or three supporting facts or examples.

Reinforce your argument by highlighting your company's flexible work policies, if it has any, and the flexible work policies of competitors and customers. Show that your request does not come out of the blue and that there are plenty of successful precedents that will weaken any counter arguments and minimize your boss's sense of risk. Keep it simple, factual and relevant.

The action plan

It is easy to promise 'improved morale, increased productivity and better communication', but how are you going to make it all work? Your action plan is about putting some substance behind your promises and showing your boss that they are not empty clichés copied from a book or downloaded off the web.

Getting your action plan right will make your idea credible. And because the action plan is all about *how* and *when*, it will also be helpful when it comes to putting your plan into action and making it work for real.

Proposal to convert the position of IT Project Manager to a compressed working week arrangement

I attach a proposal to convert my current position as IT Project Manager to a compressed working week, on a ten-hour per day, four-day per week basis.

Converting this position to a compressed working week will:

- Improve customer service, with extended office hours four days a week, at no further cost to the company.
- Improve communication with US head office, by providing a two-hour overlap time between the offices here and in New York.
- Improve productivity by providing greater blocks of time to focus on project work.
- Reduce absenteeism by improving my ability to manage external responsibilities outside working hours.

Adopting the compressed working week is consistent with company policy and industry trends:

- 'Our business encourages all parents with children six and under to adopt flexible work arrangements where possible to assist them to create balance between work and the rest of their lives' (Company Flexible Work Policy, 2003).
- A key recommendation to our clients is that they adopt family friendly initiatives to improve staff morale and reduce staff turnover. Making the theory work in practice will strengthen our argument and be considered appropriate by our clients.
- Flexible work is becoming standard industry practice, with two senior managers in two leading competitors currently in job-share arrangements.

I attach a job description, a schedule for the week showing how the arrangement will work and how it will affect the department and our clients. I have also included a brief back-up plan should there be problems with the arrangement over time.

Your action plan will include some or all of the following sections:

- Job description, including your tasks, responsibilities and performance targets.
- How the arrangement will work.
- Schedule of your availability.
- Communications plan.
- Details of your job-share partner (for job-share proposals).
- Effect on salary and benefits.
- Effect on company overheads.
- Benefits to the company.
- Process for review and evaluation.

The sections you will need to include, and the aspects you will spend more time clarifying, will depend on which flexible work option you are putting forward. Each one throws up its own opportunities and challenges and will be embraced or questioned for different reasons. Working from home might be objected to because of lack of supervision; flexitime might provoke objections on the grounds that no one will know when to expect you around the office; and job share could provoke the argument that having two people doing one job will confuse customers. Think also about the list on page 38 of reasons a company may reasonably give to refuse your flexible work arrangement. Can any of those objections be reasonably raised, and if so, what can you do to counter them? Think what specific issues your arrangement will bring up. Anticipate objections and present solutions before anyone even has a chance to raise them.

Over the following pages you will find template action plans for six flexible work options. Use the one that is right for you as the basis for your action plan. Flesh it out with facts and examples relevant to your job. Be concise and be specific.

1. Job share

Template 1

Job description. Start with your job description, listing tasks, responsibilities and performance targets. If you don't have a job description – or you don't believe the one you have is a true reflection of your responsibilities – keep a diary for a couple of weeks and record what you do, who you interact with and who depends on you to deliver your job. Your proposal needs to demonstrate that all your work will be covered under the new arrangement with no loose ends. Detailing precisely what that work entails will keep the discussion focused on achieving clear deliverables, and away from when or where the work is done.

How will the work be divided between the job-share partners? Consider each task and responsibility of the job individually and assign it to one of the two job-share partners. Try to match tasks to the partner with the most appropriate skills – but be fair. Make sure you both have equal responsibility for the more enjoyable parts of the job (the parts that get recognition and reward) and the drudge work. Use this as an opportunity to emphasize the range of skills and depth of experience that the position will draw on when there are two job-share partners filling one role.

Schedule of availability. What will your working week look like? Which one of you will be in the office when? Will there be any overlap time for handover, any joint meetings with your supervisor or other team members? If so, when and for how long?

Communications plan. Reliable communication is absolutely fundamental to a successful job-share arrangement. The two job-share partners need to communicate well between themselves. The other team members, management and customers need to know when and where to find each job-share partner, and who to talk to about which issues. Show in detail how this will work. Consider using a shared diary – electronic or otherwise – and whether a shared or separate email address and voicemail will work for your job-share team. Decide whether you should be contactable out of hours at all, in what circumstances and by whom – just your job-share partner, or by the whole team? Be realistic. Don't promise if you can't deliver.

Details of job-share partner. Wherever possible, find your job-share partner before you go to your boss to propose a job-share arrangement. Include her or his CV with a brief introductory paragraph emphasizing those skills and experience most relevant to the role and how they complement your own.

Impact on salary and benefits. Before you put your proposal together, agree with your job-share partner how you will split your pay, holiday entitlements, superannuation, sick leave and so on. Will it be straight down the middle? Talk to your human resources department if you have one. They may have previous experience of job-share arrangements and a policy already worked out.

Impact on company overheads. Consider what equipment you will need – and whether you will be able to share a computer, phone, office space, etc. What about during overlap times when you are both scheduled to be in the office? All these will have an impact on overheads and should be clarified. Again, finding out what works for other job sharers in the company is helpful.

Benefits to the organization. How will the job-share arrangement improve the value you bring to the company? What do you offer as a team that you can't offer as individuals? Think improved productivity and cutting costs. Typical business benefits of a job share might include:

- Cost savings when there is flexibility between job sharers to provide back-up for each other during busy periods, holidays or sick leave.

- More creative problem solving and better informed decision making because job-share partner's contribution will increase knowledge and experience base of the role.

- Training opportunity at no cost as job-share partners benefit from cross-fertilization of skills and experience.

Review and evaluation. Propose a trial period – say six months – for the new arrangement, with regular meetings to evaluate progress, discuss issues and fix problems. Take care to include the perspective of your colleagues and customers in the review. Make sure there are clear performance criteria against which success can be measured. Keeping them on board with the initiative will increase your chances of making it work.

Unless your company has a job-share register, the most common way to find a job-share partner is through your network.

Corrina and Vicky formed a successful job-share partnership when both were applying for the same job as a senior administrator in a small independent school. Both had considerable strengths in some aspects of the job that was vacant, but they felt that as a partnership they could offer real strength across the

Real life

I had been with the bank for more than ten years when I took 12 months' maternity leave for my first child. About three or four months before coming back I decided that I didn't want to come back full time. But when I mentioned part time the idea just met a brick wall. I phoned everyone I knew looking for a solution and eventually came up with job share.

Because I had tenure, it was easier to ask my manager to take the risk – she knew me and knew I could handle it. But the key to persuading the company was going with a partner – one who had complementary skills – and with a schedule and a communications plan. You come up against barriers when people making the decisions are without the relevant life experiences. They aren't willing to take risks with the business – until their daughter or someone close to them has been faced with the same situation. The biggest change is from a culture where work means office time to one where work is measured by output.

We set the job share up so that it was actually 1.1 of a person – we overlapped one day a week. On that day together you get twice as much done, and it ensures that nothing falls through the gaps. Just being able to collaborate with someone else is brilliant. We go through a notebook each month. Auditors just love job-share positions because every little thing is documented – which is great from a compliance perspective.

You have to be thick skinned in terms of other people's views because there are still people who think that you have got an easy ride – that somehow you are not pulling your weight. At the end of the day it's the quality of work and your output that matter. The only opinion you need to worry about is your own: 'Am I doing my job properly?' You'll know in your heart if you are and bad luck to everyone else's perceptions. After all, when a job share is working well you can do more in three days than others do in five.

For me, the key to the success of the job share is that I start at eight, finish at five three days a week – and while I am there the bank gets 150 per cent.

Melinda, financial services, two children

skills required, and some more beyond. They joined forces and presented themselves as a team. It took more than three months to negotiate the final detail. Job sharing was new to the school and there were many who had to be convinced. Three years later, the school certainly feels it got two and more for the price of one, and both job sharers are enjoying the flexibility and the mutual support that the arrangement gives them.

Peta, in financial services, found her job-share partner by maintaining contacts with work colleagues while on maternity leave. An opportunity came up when a work colleague suggested the idea of job sharing. She thought they would make a good team. Based on that recommendation, they put together a proposal and it was taken on board.

What to look for in a job-share partner

1   Can they do the work? Do they have the skills, experience and qualifications that the job needs?

2   Do they share your attitude and willingness to make the job share work?

3   Do they have good communication skills? A successful job share is often keeping the sharing seamless from the outsider's point of view. So a willingness to share information, be honest about issues that arise and be able to negotiate effectively, together with good written and verbal communication skills, can really help make a job share work.

4   Do they have any complementary skills or qualifications that will broaden and enhance what you bring to the role as a team over what you bring to the role on your own?

5   Do you have a similar work ethic? Can you reconcile your different working styles to your mutual benefit? Or will they become a source of conflict?

6   Can you envisage this person as your friend? You are going to be working very closely together so you need to be able to trust each other and rely on each other.

7   Can your timetables be made to work for both of you?

2. Working from home

The most common reason why employers refuse requests to work from home is that they do not consider the work can be done without supervision. The cost to set up a work space at your home may also be a reason for objection if you need complex equipment and the company is to fund it. Keep these objections in mind as you put your case together for working from home. Also keep in mind that AT&T has turned 50,000 US employees into telecommuters, resulting in an annual saving of US$80 million in overheads.

Template 2

Job description. Start with your job description, listing tasks, responsibilities and performance targets. If you don't have a job description – or you don't believe the one you have is a true reflection of your responsibilities – keep a diary for a couple of weeks and record what you do, who you interact with and who depends on you to deliver your job. Your proposal needs to demonstrate that all your work will be covered under the new arrangement with no loose ends. Precise details on what that work requires will keep the discussion focused on achieving clear deliverables, and away from when or where the work is done.

What will working from home mean for your job? List the tasks you plan to do at home and why they are especially suited for working from home – for example, work that doesn't require constant input from others, work that needs spans of concentration or work that you simply need to spread out all over your living room floor to get to grips with. Also list the tasks that you will continue to do in the office. Show what proportion of your working week each represents and how that is reflected in your working from home schedule.

Schedule of availability. Be clear about what your working week will look like. Include the following:

- How often you propose to work from home.
- Whether it will change weekly depending on the nature of your work or whether it will be a regular timetable with, say, two specific days.

- How work from home time will fit around regular team meetings, client liaison, management meetings and any other workplace based activity.

Communications plan. How you will stay in regular contact is important if you are planning to work off-site. Be clear about how and when communication will take place. Propose regular timetabled briefings and progress reviews. For example: 9am phone call with manager to brief on day's priorities, or email update at 5pm on progress and priorities for the following day. A broadband connection and the ability to access remotely your company's network will make file sharing and communicating with team members more seamless. Conference calling will allow you to take part in team meetings. Include details on how you will be contactable at home by team members, clients, etc.

Work environment and equipment. Your employer will need to know that you have an appropriate working environment where you can do your job safely and effectively. You will need to detail set-up requirements, including computer hardware, software licensing, extra phone line, broadband, voicemail, etc. The organization will need to consider cost, liability and so forth, and may require a health and safety visit to your home. Speak to your human resources department if you have one to find out whether there are any policies or precedents for work at home agreements. Advice on putting together a working from home agreement is available from the Institute of Directors' information sheet, 'Employees who work from home', at www.IOD.com.

Impact on company overheads. Overall, working from home arrangements are considered an opportunity to reduce overheads and use existing office space and equipment more effectively – stress this if it is the case.

Benefits to the organization. How will the working from home arrangement benefit the company? Think improved productivity and cutting costs. Typical benefits might include:

- Increased productivity because all work that needs focused periods of concentration can be done away from the busy office environment without interruption.

- Improved quality of work – better able to concentrate and starting work fresh and early two days a week without tackling the traffic or public transport.
- Reducing company overheads by releasing valuable office space for use by others for parts of the week.

Review and evaluation. Propose a trial period – say six months – for the new arrangement, with regular meetings to evaluate progress, discuss issues and fix problems. Take care to include the perspective of your colleagues and customers in the review. Make sure there are clear performance criteria against which success can be measured. Keeping them on board with the initiative will increase your chances of making it work.

Real life

Working at home allowed me to breastfeed both my children until they were one and I haven't had to put either into long day care, which I haven't wanted to.

But working from home has its difficulties. For example, if I have a meeting, I have to go out – I can't just run down the hall for a quick meeting, so it can take a substantial chunk of my working time. I tried having an author meeting at home when Connor was very little because I couldn't get a babysitter. It didn't work. He didn't play quietly in the background of course, so it didn't feel very professional. Sometimes I have to meet authors at a difficult time for mothering – say four o'clock in the afternoon. It's not ideal.

I am contracted to work two days a week and I find I might work two days plus a few evenings and nap times on 'non-working days'. When both children are at school I will work back in the office. The arrangement has worked for me while the children are small, but I would prefer to separate my working life from my family life now.

Angela, publishing, two children

3. Compressed working week

This is a creative solution to keeping a full-time job by squeezing it into fewer days so you have time off during the week for family

TABLE 2.1: Working from home dos and don'ts

Do	Don't
DO make sure that expectations of what you are going to do at home are agreed and clear.	DON'T be fooled into thinking that working from home is a substitute for childcare. It isn't.
DO make sure you have an appropriate space to work in and the right equipment to do the job.	DON'T let yourself get isolated from your colleagues.
DO stay in regular touch with your peers: schedule time at the office when you can participate in team meetings; maintain some social contact if possible; access the company intranet or LAN to stay abreast of company developments, training opportunities and internal vacancies.	DON'T forget to give yourself proper breaks, for lunch, to stretch, etc.
	DON'T let the office think 'out of sight, out of mind'. Remind them of your presence and your valuable contribution at every opportunity.
	DON'T forget to get involved with extra curricula work activities such as being on a work health and safety committee, getting involved in business planning, etc. This will remind people you are available, consolidate your role in the team and expose you to business issues beyond your specific daily tasks and projects.
DO keep clear divisions between working time and home time. If you work at home it is much more difficult to 'leave work at the office' at the end of the day.	DON'T hesitate to ask for help when you need it.
DO establish an agreed reporting in plan with your manager, and stick to it. It is as much for your benefit as for theirs. It will be a good way of checking your own progress and developing work satisfaction and sense of achievement.	

and other hobbies. On the upside, you get to keep your status, professional responsibilities and salary. On the downside, you will be squeezing a full week's worth of work, and working hours, into four days or fewer. This may leave you so exhausted that you are fit for nothing much on the precious day you have earned for yourself at home.

You will need to persuade your employer that you can be effective when working long shifts – ten hours, or even 12 if you attempt to squeeze your work into three days. They may also want to be convinced about how you will track your time when working extended hours.

Template 3

Job description. List your tasks, responsibilities and performance targets. If you don't have a job description – or you don't believe the one you have is a true reflection of your responsibilities – keep a diary for a couple of weeks and record what you do, who you interact with and who depends on you to deliver your job. Your proposal needs to demonstrate that all your work will be covered under the new arrangement with no loose ends and that performance targets will be met. Detailing precisely what that work entails will keep the discussion focused on achieving clear deliverables, and away from when or where the work is done.

How will you get your work done in a compressed working week? List those responsibilities which can be done effectively outside of working hours. Show why these might be particularly suited to being done at that time – ability to concentrate better, cross-over with office hours of overseas based business relationships, etc.

Schedule of availability. Will the day you take off each week be the same? Or will it vary depending on work commitments? The same day will allow people to adjust to a pattern of absence. Different days may give you and the employer more flexibility but may be more disruptive to colleagues. Ensure that your out-of-office days do not coincide with scheduled meetings or work that relies on face to face contact. Consider the impact your altered timetable will have on colleagues and whether anyone needs to adjust their work patterns and expectations to allow you to work a compressed week. Detail your proposed timetable, with arrival and departure times. Ensure that you will have access to the premises at those times. If you feel it will help your boss to accept the idea, propose a form of sign-in/sign-out sheet so that your hours can be monitored.

Communications plan. This will be important if your schedule varies frequently. How will people know when you will be available? It will also be an issue if the day off means you miss important regular team meetings. Ensure there is communication of everything that happens when you are out of the office, so that you remain in the loop and can follow up as necessary during your office hours. Decide whether you should be contactable out of hours at all, in what circumstances and by whom. Be realistic – don't promise if you can't deliver.

Work environment and equipment. Verify that your equipment and office space will be available and accessible during the proposed extended hours. If you think someone else could benefit from your workspace and equipment on your days off, say so.

Impact on salary and benefits. Since you are proposing to do your full-time job in a compressed week, there should be no impact on your salary or benefits, so do not include this.

Impact on company overheads. You may be able to argue a reduction in overheads if your office space and equipment can be effectively used by someone else when you are out of the office.

Benefits to the organization. Consider what benefits your compressed working week will bring to the company. These might include:

- Better coverage of customer needs due to extended office hours, at no extra cost.
- Increased efficiency due to bigger blocks of time being available to work on projects.
- Increased productivity because projects that need concentration and uninterrupted time can be done outside of normal office hours when there are fewer interruptions.
- Improved liaison with overseas customers and suppliers because extended office hours means greater overlap with different business time zones.

Review and evaluation. Propose a trial period (for example, six months) for the new arrangement with regular meetings to evaluate progress, discuss issues and fix problems. Make sure there are clear performance criteria against which success can be measured. Take care to include the perspective of your colleagues and customers in the review. Keeping them on board with the initiative will increase your chances of making it work.

Real life

I negotiated a compressed working week with the bank I work for – keeping a full-time job with four days' work, and one day a week at home – although I am available online. It works because my husband is able to be flexible with his work – he has his own business and works four days a week. When I was able to persuade him to work fewer hours it was a real turning point for all of us. I have a sister and my mother living nearby – and that is a great backstop too. They can sometimes take the children after school and my husband can pick them up around six and bring them home. I can get home and spend an hour with them before they go to bed.

I have to make every hour in the office fruitful – every waking hour count. I am much, much more efficient. After dinner in the evening I do an hour or so's work – emails and calls to our overseas offices.

The 12 weeks of school holidays are always difficult – and there is always a question about whether you are short changing the children, but the opportunity cost of not working is high. And with both of us on a four-day week it is working well.

The trick is not to be too available, to keep work in perspective and to stay fit and healthy. As a mother you play a central role in the household – if you are not happy, everyone picks up on it. If you lose your health you can go under – it will affect your work, your children and put strain on your marriage.

Lyn, financial services, two children

4. Flexitime

Flexitime is a widely accepted work practice and means flexible start and finish times (usually with the option of bankable hours, where any overtime you work during one period can be taken as time in lieu during quieter periods). Many public service workers have flexitime agreements formalized in their awards. It also works successfully on an informal basis in many workplaces. An informal arrangement is great and, when it works well, it cuts the paper-work down and creates a feeling of goodwill and trust. However, it may be worth having a written arrangement in the long term.

If your manager changes or the company gets taken over, an informal arrangement can be forgotten easily.

Template 4

Job description. List your tasks, responsibilities and performance targets. If you don't have a job description – or you don't believe the one you have is a true reflection of your responsibilities – keep a diary for a couple of weeks and record what you do, who you interact with and who depends on you to deliver your job. Your proposal needs to demonstrate that all your work will be covered under the new arrangement with no loose ends and that performance targets will be met. Detailing precisely what that work entails will keep the discussion focused on achieving clear deliverables, and away from when or where the work is done.

Schedule of availability. A successful flexitime arrangement is all about scheduling. So this section is the crux of your argument. Propose core hours during the day during which you'll be in the office; 10am–3.30pm is common, but does it suit your job? Tailor them to suit the work you do. When are peak customer contact hours? When do most team meetings happen? Consider too how any time in lieu that you accrue by working extra hours will be managed to fit with low periods of business activity. Finally, since a flexitime arrangement depends on accurately counting hours at work, you will need to come up with a time sheet or sign-in process that you and your boss can work with.

Benefits to the organization. How will the flexitime arrangement increase the value you bring to the company? Typical benefits might include:

● Reduced overtime bill because you are able to organize your work to cover busy periods and take time off during less busy periods.
● Improved customer service with core hours tailored to customer requirements.
● Reduced absenteeism because you are better able to schedule family business outside of work hours.

Review and evaluation. Propose a trial period – say six months – for the new arrangement, with regular meetings to evaluate progress, discuss issues and fix problems. Make sure there are clear performance criteria against which success can be measured. Take care to include the perspective of your colleagues and customers in the review. Keeping them on board with the initiative will increase your chances of making it work.

Real life

The academic world is easy for juggling – with the public service conditions and culture. You are working with people who are politically progressive (despite the glass ceiling – there still aren't many women at professor level). People tend to be open-minded. And we have public service conditions. I have to be here for the students, but with flexitime I can arrive at 7.30 and go home at 4.30. So, even though my partner is the primary carer, ultimately I am also involved in the childcare and I can do the 5 'til 8 shift every evening.

Catharine, academic and journalist, two children

5. Term-time only work

A term-time only contract is a dream arrangement for many mothers, but it is not common outside of educational organizations. It can be made to work in all kinds of jobs, however. The key is to persuade your employer to focus on outcomes for the whole year, or the financial quarter, rather than what gets done day to day. Work that is project based, or seasonal, is particularly suitable.

To make a strong case for a term-time only contract, you will need to show that your principal work activities can be managed on a 40-week calendar. You will also need to demonstrate that you are organized, motivated and goal oriented, can be relied on to meet all project requirements and have plans in place for coverage during leave periods.

Template 5

Job description. List your tasks, responsibilities and performance targets. If you don't have a job description – or you don't believe the one you have is a true reflection of your responsibilities – keep a diary for a couple of weeks and record what you do, who you interact with and who depends on you to deliver your job. Your proposal needs to demonstrate that all your work will be covered under the new arrangement with no loose ends and that performance targets will be met. Detailing precisely what that work entails will keep the discussion focused on achieving clear deliverables, and away from when or where the work is done.

How will the work be done under the new arrangement? Is your work project based, and predictable, so that it can be scheduled to occur in specific time frames? If not, what plans can you put in place for coverage during leave time? How will ongoing problem solving or crisis management of your work be managed while you are absent?

Schedule of availability. You should be able to provide term-time dates a year in advance. Will you be completely unavailable during holiday periods? Are there circumstances in which you will be contactable? Under which circumstances and by whom?

Communications plan. If you are going to be contactable during the holiday periods, ensure all contact details are up to date.

Work environment and equipment. Will your work equipment and space be available for others during leave periods?

Impact on salary and benefits. Like a part-time role, the most acceptable arrangement will be a pro-rata rate of your full-time salary. You could ask for payments to be spread as a regular monthly salary throughout the year, giving you a lower but continuous cash flow, or be paid only during term times. A term-time only contract will normally stipulate that any paid leave due be taken during the school holidays.

Impact on company overheads. There is potential to reduce overheads if equipment can be used by others while you are on leave.

Benefits to the organization. How will term-time only work increase the value you bring to the organization? Think improved productivity and cutting costs. It is useful in roles with lower demand during school holidays or for project work.

Review and evaluation. Propose a trial period – say six months – for the new arrangement, with regular meetings to evaluate progress, discuss issues and fix problems. Make sure there are clear performance criteria against which success can be measured. Take care to include the perspective of your colleagues and customers in the review. Keeping them on board with the initiative will increase your chances of making it work.

Real life

Before I had Phoebe, I was with a travel agent for 12 years. I was happy there, and saw myself staying, working my way up through management. But once I had had a baby everything changed. I became much more aware of the inflexible hours – you were expected to work evenings, weekends, there was no question of only working term time, no understanding of what I was looking for – being able to spend more time with my daughter. So I decided to look around for something else. I saw a position advertised with the Norwich and Peterborough Building Society that interested me so I rang and asked for an application form. But it was a full-time job – and I could see that it needed to be full time. I left it and didn't think more about it until the building society called me to ask why I hadn't applied. I was very honest – I said that I appreciated that it needed to be full time and that I was looking for something that would allow me time off during school holidays. They said 'leave it with us' and I thought that would be the last I would hear from them. But two days later they called back and said they could create a position for me.

There are plenty of mothers on the team, so there is real understanding of what makes things easy. We more or less negotiate our hours between us – always so it works for the business of course. I work 9 'til 3 and only during the school term. There are three of us on term-time only contracts. I get sent on training courses, and I am part of a career progression scheme that sets goals and allows me to move up the ladder. It gives me something to aim for and a sense of achievement. I'm paid pro rata over 12 months which means I'm not left without a pay cheque during the long summer break.

In terms of self-development, over time I might like something more. But for now I am very satisfied.

Claire, customer service, one child

6. Annualized hours

A strong case can be made for annualized hours where business has seasonal ebbs and flows. For employers who traditionally use casual workers at different times during the year, an annualized hours agreement can extend that relationship to a permanent position, without the overheads of keeping someone on year round when there is less work.

Working time regulations state that you should not be forced to work more than 48 hours in a working week, unless you opt out or work in exempted professions or industry. This should be taken into account when structuring the ebb and flow of annualized hours worked.

Template 6

Job description. List your tasks, responsibilities and performance targets. If you don't have a job description – or you don't believe the one you have is a true reflection of your responsibilities – keep a diary for a couple of weeks and record what you do, who you interact with and who depends on you to deliver your job. Your proposal needs to demonstrate that all your work will be covered under the new arrangement with no loose ends and that performance targets will be met. Detailing precisely what that work entails will keep the discussion focused on achieving clear deliverables, and away from when or where the work is done.

Schedule of availability. Show you will be available during peak periods of demand. Can you be available at other times, and how much notice do you need? If total number of hours are worked before the end of the year, will you be available for extra work (charged separately)? Annualized hours agreements may have a cap to the number of hours that can be worked during a given week for health and safety reasons.

Communications plan. During periods of low demand, how will you be contactable?

Work environment and equipment. Will need to be provided during work times only.

Impact on salary and benefits. You can agree to have a regular monthly salary paid, equal to the total hours scheduled for the year, divided by 12, regardless of hours worked during the specific month.

Impact on company overheads. This arrangement reduces the cost of employing contract workers repeatedly (search and selection). Also, since contract and casual workers often work at a premium to offset disadvantages of irregularity and unpredictability of employment, annualized hours may reduce the salary bill. Payroll costs are also reduced because there is less need to calculate considerable fluctuations in weekly costs and benefits.

Benefits to the organization. How will an annualized hours arrangement increase the value you bring to the company? Some benefits from annualized hours might include:

- The creation of an ongoing relationship with seasonal workers, so retaining company knowledge and expertise.
- Increased efficiency and less time spent and cost incurred in search and selection process for casuals each peak season.
- Increased value of training staff, because they are going to be around longer.
- It ensures permanent staff are available for peak periods, without the cost of paying them for the full year.
- Reduction in payroll costs because the organization can manage cash flow for salaries across a 12-month period rather than in erratic peaks and troughs.

Review and evaluation. Propose a trial period – say six months – for the new arrangement, with regular meetings to evaluate progress, discuss issues and fix problems. Make sure there are clear performance criteria against which success can be measured. Take care to include the perspective of your colleagues and customers in the review. Keeping them on board with the initiative will increase your chances of making it work.

Step 4: Present your proposal

Making a strong case is, of course, a lot to do with presentation. After all, we know that we all judge books by their cover. When

The Peak District National Parks Authority has negotiated a range of flexible work arrangements with employees, including annualized hours contracts. In the words of one employee:

'I hate travelling to and from work in the dark and prefer to work fewer hours in the winter. At the same time, the workload of my team has a big peak from April to June while between December and February we're quieter. So it made sense for me to adopt an annualized hours scheme where I work a 32-hour week in January and February, 37 hours during the two weeks either side and 38 hours for the remaining 40 weeks. I've been through my first winter using the scheme and I've found it really liberating. It suits my natural rhythms and it also matches my workload pattern.'

Courtesy of Swiftwork, Flexible Working Consultants

you have researched and put together your plan, spend a little time making it look as professional as it reads. You want the finished document to be comprehensive but also easy for someone to find their way around and get to the parts that they are most interested in.

- Check your wording. Is it clear and concise? Have you avoided repetition?
- Look at the structure. If you have used the headings suggested in this chapter, is everything logically placed?
- Check the layout. Are the headings clear, and is each section well spaced? Is it easy to follow the flow of the document? Is there plenty of white space? Have you numbered the pages and put footers on each, with the title, date and your name?
- Do a test print out. Do the printed pages work? Do the page breaks happen in logical places?
- Do you have all the attachments you need? For example, your job sharer's CV, your CV and your executive summary?

Choose your moment

Choose the moment that you present your request carefully. Be sensitive to what is going on in the business. This doesn't just mean avoiding the bad times, when people are tired or work isn't going well. Is there anything going on which you can use to support your case? Maybe a big overtime bill has come in and you can show how your flexitime proposal will help keep that down or perhaps a new customer contact opportunity has been identified between 5pm and 7pm when the office is usually shut. This could helpfully support your proposal for extended shifts and a compressed working week.

What is a good time?

You know your boss better than anyone. But often a good time to get a busy person's attention is just outside office hours, when the phone isn't ringing so much and there are fewer interruptions. Try just before work, at lunchtime or at the end of the business day.

You may want to introduce the idea, hand over the document and make a time to discuss it in detail, but striking while the iron is hot is a pretty sound strategy. If you have their attention, seize the moment, then make your case with confidence!

What if the answer is 'no'?

This will be most unsatisfactory – but, of course, doesn't have to mean the end of the road for your flexible work idea. First, as long as your child is under six (or under 18 if he or she has a disability), your employer can refuse only on clear business grounds. See page 38. If you have argued your case in the business context, you will have anticipated and accounted for any business issues.

Make sure you clearly understand your manager's grounds for saying 'no'. Once both you and your employer have all your cards on the table, negotiating your way to a mutually satisfactory solution will be clearer. In most situations it is safe to assume that your boss does not want to lose you. Recruiting new staff is expensive and time consuming. It is in the organization's interests that you stay.

If an employer refuses a reasonable request for flexible work, there is a procedure that should be followed. This includes an opportunity to appeal. The Department of Trade and Industry has outlined this procedure very clearly in its booklet 'Flexible working: the right to request and the duty to consider. A guide for employers and employees', which can be downloaded from the website, www.dti.gov.uk. Lapses in procedure can be taken to ACAS or to an employment tribunal.

Real life

When I got back from maternity leave, a group of us got together socially one day. We were all women, all either with young children or thinking about having a family. We started talking about things we wanted to see change – and being able to work flexibly when you have young children sparked everyone's passion. Our social group became a working group to make it happen which then expanded to include a number of men who were job sharing for various reasons other than supporting families. We were supported in our endeavours by our organization which was committed to a focus on diversity – we were ready and we caught the wave.

Peta, financial services, two children

Section 2

Finding and getting the job you want

3

Making a start if it's been a long time

No one likes looking for a job – it's daunting at the best of times. When you have been away from work looking after children for any length of time, the prospect of a job hunt can be truly nerve-racking.

After all, from the moment we find out we are pregnant we begin to talk ourselves out of believing that we could ever do a decent job again. We start with amusing stories of finding the car keys in the oven or walking into Sainsbury's and completely forgetting what we are there for. And for a time, we wear 'nappy brain' or 'preg head' as our 'new mother's badge of honour'. But as time wears on, and pregnancy hormones give way to sleep deprivation, and sleep deprivation makes room for the stress of the family juggle, we can have totally talked ourselves out of being able to string together a coherent sentence, let alone being taken seriously at a job interview.

Kate Winslet did it: 'I really did suffer this thing of pregnancy dementia and I have not really got my brain back. It's really scary arriving at work and thinking "Bloody hell! Where have these lines gone?"' But at least she's got a job to go to.

A government commissioned report has shown that mothers have a harder time finding work than any other social group. It's toughest for mothers of young children but, according to the figures, things don't get much easier as children get older.

And without doubt, the longer you have been out of the workforce, the more of a struggle the job market is likely to be.

Real life

I don't know where to start looking for work. Five years out and three children and I feel completely unemployable. My contacts have all dated and I feel right out of touch with what is going on the industry – the buzzwords, everything.

Before I took maternity leave I was offered a role as head of marketing for the Asia-Pac region with a global telecoms company. Now I think, who would hire me?

I used to earn more than my partner, and now I don't know what I want to do or where to start – and with a day that starts at 5.20am and finishes with sleep by nine at night, there is very little time for myself or to really think these things through.

Jane, international marketing, IT and media, three children

So much about finding the right job is about how you feel about yourself: having the confidence to work out what you want to do, and believing that you are capable of doing it; being self-assured enough to sell your idea to others – potential employers, customers, even those around you; having the courage to put your plan into action and to stick with it.

Then there is the job hunt itself – a process so evidently complex that it has spawned a multi-billion dollar global industry to teach us how to find a great job, create a winning CV, a triumphant covering letter and be victorious in an interview.

Do we feel like getting out there and selling ourselves on the job market – marketing our skills and promoting our attributes like they tell us we have to? Not necessarily. We can feel like crawling back under the baby's cot and curling up for a while among discarded toys and bottles of rancid milk.

Why? Because to get a job we need to compete in the world outside and we have been very focused for a period on the home and family. Becoming a parent is an incredible opportunity to learn new skills, develop different understandings and grow in new ways – but you can bet no one is going to ask about all that in a job interview.

When you go for a job, you know that you will be judged by a set of criteria that you had put aside, at least for a time. It doesn't mean you won't match up once you get out there, but getting out there and putting yourself on the line takes a bit of extra courage for many of us.

By putting yourself back into the job market you are exposing yourself to risk. And it is unsettling. There is a lot we could choose to be concerned about: failure, rejection, change, competing with others, being evaluated by employers who don't know you, asking for something for yourself, being told you are too old, too experienced or not experienced enough.

And you could even be worried about succeeding – getting the job and having to leave the children and go out to work: the adjustment, the juggling, the guilt and the very venture into the unknown that that would mean.

But at the same time you are ready for new challenges, and almost certainly ready for a pay cheque. So, if you are feeling a little shaky about getting started on the job search, what do you do?

Where to start

If it has been a long time since you last had a job – not since 'mobiles' were phones with long leads that reached into the next room – then it's all right to approach your return to work slowly. At least to begin with. You can take over the world next month.

The biggest shift is going to be in your mind – from domestic goddess to working woman – and in the minds of all the people around you, starting with the ones who are used to having you at home, available day and night, to drop off, pick up, cook, shop for, study with, play with, talk to, listen to, sing to and to pick up their shirts from the dry cleaners 'if you're not busy, please ...'.

Start thinking yourself back into work. This means stop being available 24/7, organize the time and tools you will need and start spending more time with other people who are working.

Give yourself as long a lead time as you can afford. Browse the job ads to get a feel for what is out there. Don't feel you have to find something that interests you right away.

Set aside time each week. This should be at least two hours, longer if you can. Not time when you are doing other things like

I have been browsing the job bulletin boards for the past year. I have now started to find things that sound pretty interesting. Now I just have to pull together a résumé. After 11 years I'm pretty rusty.

Kim, bulletin board, babiestoday.com

hanging out the washing or driving someone somewhere. Time when you won't be interrupted, when you are not available. Use this to think about your job search – what you want to do and how you plan to approach it.

Find somewhere to work. A spare corner of the house will do, but getting out to the library, a coffee shop or even a friend's place will help create a division between home and work, and you won't be tempted by the many alluring distractions of housework.

Dress the part. Make sure you have a work-appropriate outfit that fits – yes even around your waist – has no sticky finger marks on it (black is good) and isn't completely out of date. Borrow or buy a suit. Put it on, tuck a folded newspaper under your arm and head off to your workplace.

Get the equipment. A mobile phone is a necessity not a luxury. If you can, keep the number only for professional contacts. That way, whenever it rings you'll know it is a business call – and shouldn't be answered until you have given your three year old a whole box of chocolate biscuits to keep her happy, your seventeen year old the keys to the car and turned on the television for anyone in between. Then you can confidently take the call in your calm and in-control professional voice and not fear being interrupted for at least 73 seconds.

Internet access and your own email address are equally essential. The internet is a key job search tool, not just to register with the employment databases, but for background research into different industries, companies, etc. Make sure you have your own email address – a shared address or one in your partner's name, for example, may leave the impression that you are shy of computers and the internet.

Have business cards printed. Include your name, mobile number and email address – home phone number too if you like. This does not need to be expensive and will add to your sense of yourself as a woman with a foot in the world of work. It will also be invaluable as you start to build up your network of job-search related contacts.

Do lunch. Get in touch with people you used to work with and meet them for lunch or a drink after work. Get the gossip on the place you used to work, and on the state of the industry. If you have lost contact with former colleagues, do you know anyone who works in an environment similar to the one you used to work in, or would like to work in? Meet up with them.

Surround yourself with supporters. Start with your partner, and let them know how they can help. How are you introduced at parties? 'This is Kim, my partner, and mother to our 16 beautiful children.' How about slipping 'this is Kim, she has a background in mineral engineering and has many years' experience on North Sea oil rigs' into a conversation with the neighbours about the price of fish? I am not for a moment suggesting that you should stop talking about your children or property prices over Sunday lunch, but reminding yourself and others who you are and what you have achieved apart from the 16 children will increase your professional confidence and confirm you on the path to your next career goals.

Consider voluntary work. This will help to update your skills, increase your exposure to work related issues and broaden your network of contacts (see Chapter 7).

Research upskilling and retraining opportunities. There is a range of courses that look at the general issues surrounding transition back to work (see Chapter 1). As you become closer to understanding where your interests lie you can consider vocational courses. Look at continuing education programmes run by adult education bodies, technical colleges and universities in your area. Contact relevant professional associations to find out what professional development programmes they run.

Kick starting your confidence

Confidence is key to getting what you want. And confidence is what you will need when it comes to talking your way into a great job or a completely new industry, especially when you have spent

Real life

People who have been constantly in the workforce underestimate how much it takes to get back to work. If you have stayed out of work until your second child, say, has started school, it is an awfully long time. Volunteering is a non-confronting way to start juggling timetables and other demands – getting the children to school, getting yourself somewhere on public transport and turning up somewhere when people expect and need you to be there. Volunteering is a safe way to rebuild these basic skills.

Volunteering is a good way to maintain your skills while you are out of the workforce, to develop new skills and test being back at work. Confidence is critical. Confidence is linked to self-esteem, especially if you have been relegated to 'I am just at home with the children'. Pay can be irrelevant if you find an interesting role, doing something that other people value, and you find value in yourself. It can really build your confidence.

Sha, volunteer worker, two children

the last three years loading and unloading the dishwasher, changing nappies and asking people not to keep leaving their clothes all over the place – do they think this is a hotel, for good-ness sake?

Diminished confidence is common among so many women who have taken extended leave from work to be at home with the children. It's not personal confidence they lack, but confidence in their professional selves seems to desert so many women when they step out of work for a while.

It is an easy trap to fall into: you lose confidence in yourself, you lower your expectations, you undersell yourself, you accept poorer terms and conditions than you would have ever dreamt of. You might believe that you've traded in or even traded *up* for flexi-bility and that the compromise is inevitable, but hang on. Childbirth can be a messy operation – and leave some ugly scars, I can tell you – but it isn't a lobotomy. Nor does it rob you of who you were or what you achieved in the past. If you have a law degree, going part time doesn't make that half a law degree. If you have global business experience, taking two years out doesn't take away what you know about international affairs. You might need to update, of course, but the world hasn't fundamentally changed while you've been focused elsewhere. Once you get back to work, even the office gossip can sound drearily familiar.

It depends on your industry, of course, but for many of us, so much of what we missed when we were taking DIY lessons from Bob the Builder can actually be made up after a couple of months back in the working environment, a few days at the computer brushing up on – or learning from scratch – some software packages and catching up with colleagues and peers over lunch or a drink after work.

Real life

During the three years I was at home with the children email totally took off. On my first day back at work – in a completely new job – I was just terrified they'd find out that I couldn't use it and they'd sack me on the spot. I remember sitting there at the computer, rigid, looking at the clock – and working out the timings. It was nine-thirty. They'd probably catch on by eleven, fire me by about eleven-thirty and I'd be home for twelve. I didn't think there was any point in making a start on any of the work they'd ask me to do, because I'd be gone by lunchtime. 'I'll just sit here and wait,' I thought. They didn't sack me, of course, and I now run the lab that hired me – and all the computer equipment in it, of course.

Fiona, lab technician, two children

But while so many women on the point of going back to work talk about the loss of confidence, the other side of it is that so many say that they are surprised how quickly confidence returns once they are back in the working environment, doing what they are good at, being treated like professionals and surrounded by people none of whom needs their nappy changed.

It can feel like a catch-22 – you'll get confidence once you are back working, but to get back to work you need confidence.

Confidence building strategies

1   Think positively. It's a cliché, but it is so easy to be hard on
    yourself and to dwell on all the things that you believe are
    stopping you get what you want. If you spend a little more
    time cheering yourself on and less time selling yourself short
    you might start believing it. And the quickest way to
    convince others that you've got what it takes is to convince
    yourself.

2   Spend time with people who think you are fantastic. Positive
    self-talk is one thing, but it helps if the people around you
    agree that you are a talent-soaked, skill-loaded, insightful
    person with scientific understanding and artistic abundance
    who has only to choose a path to be successful.

3   Remember your past successes – remember how they made
    you feel. Try to conjure up that feeling whenever you are
    faced with a challenge.

4   Write down the good stuff about yourself – what you believe
    in, what your goals are, what is fabulous about who you are.
    Writing things down is a great way of reinforcing them.
    Don't be timid with the compliments.

5   When things go wrong (and they will), find the funny side.
    There is one.

6   Break down any task that you find daunting into small steps.
    Get a sense of achievement for each step you complete
    successfully.

7   Reward yourself for your successes – even the small ones to
    start off with.

8   When things *do* go wrong, remind yourself of the bits that
    went right.

9   If you feel good about yourself, you will feel more confident.
    So put on a bit of lipstick, get to the gym, dress confidently –
    whatever it is that puts a smile on your face.

But above all remember, to get the job you want you don't have to
be confident, you just have to make them think you are. As long
as you can look them in the eye, and answer questions with an

unwavering confident smile during the interview, you can dissolve into blubbering jelly as soon as you have got out of the building, walked down the street and around the corner.

When it was my time to launch myself back into work, I was energetic, optimistic and a little naive. Mark, my partner, took a couple of weeks off work to give me some time and space to kick things into gear, and the job hunt was on. I was pretty sure that by the time his leave was over, I would be in the process of considering a couple of tempting options – flexible work with a fabulous view and no commute – oh, and the pay would be good too!

I decided that I couldn't sit at home mulling over the job ads and sipping coffee while he got to grips with the children, tempting though it was. I had to get out of the house and leave him and the children to muddle their way through it – even if it meant, as I suspected, the girls wearing their clothes back to front and their nappies on their heads.

I took my first day very seriously indeed. I dressed for the office. I kissed the girls goodbye at the door and felt so proud and so liberated as I headed to the bus stop, walking backwards most of the way so that I could keep waving at them – just as Mark did most mornings, when it was me standing on the doorstep. This is the kind of mother I want for my daughters, I thought. At last, this is the role model I want to create – a working mother, a woman stimulated and excited by her contribution to the world beyond hearth and home, but a woman committed and fulfilled by her relationships with her family and the joy she takes in bringing up her children.

I felt I had it all.

I didn't, of course, I had a copy of the *Financial Times* and a weekly bus ticket, but I didn't have a job.

When I didn't have a job by the time Mark's leave was over and he headed back to work, I wasn't worried. I had registered with a couple of agencies and with all the online job search sites. I was receiving vacancy listings in my inbox every day. A couple of times a week I would be moved to fire off an application or two. None was for the job of my dreams, but no matter, a bit of interview practice would hone my skills and give me a deeper understanding of the market when it came to applying for a job that I really wanted.

In fact, although I had at least made a start, I had a lot to learn about working out what I really wanted, and how to sell myself before my return to work even began to be successful.

Now that you have made a start with your job hunt and are beginning to feel confident about what you are going to achieve, the next step is to find the right opportunity for you to get back to work.

4

Where to look for the right job for you

Now that you have a clear picture in your mind of the kind of work you are looking for, how are you going to find it?

Here is the advice most careers advisers will give to people who are looking for work:

1 Make the most of your network; most jobs come through your own professional network – who you know *really* matters.

2 Go direct – choose a company that you would love to work for and give them a call. Find out if they are hiring. Let them know about you.

3 Approach the employment agencies.

4 As a last resort, look at the job classifieds.

But you are not just *anyone* looking for work, you are now a working mother – you have just had a few months at home honing your nappy changing skills, or maybe a couple of years perfecting your parenting prowess. The normal advice doesn't apply – in fact it sounds something like this:

My network? I have been out of the system too long, everyone I used to know has moved on – or retired.

Approach the companies? What me? Call Goldman Sachs/Saatchi & Saatchi/Big Brother's production company, and just let them know I am available? Nah – they'd laugh at me. What would I say? I bet they wouldn't even return my call.

The agencies? That doesn't work. They don't want people like me. They never advertise part-time work and they don't understand my skills. They keep putting me up for admin jobs.

The job classifieds? Ah, that's where I feel comfortable, browsing the job pages with a coffee on a Saturday morning, mentally applying for all kinds of exciting opportunities, anonymously putting my hand up for roles and responsibilities that meet my wildest dreams; searching online databases of tens of thousands of jobs in exotic locations and receiving emailed updates of positions tailored to my skills and experience. But no, I don't usually send in my CV.

According to government statistics for 2002, networking is the most successful way to find a job. Answering job ads comes second, cold calling – approaching a company on spec to see if they might have a vacancy – is third, while the fourth most successful way to find a job is going through a recruitment agent.

So, if like me you are inclined to focus on the ads and the agencies when you look for work and avoid calling companies cold, or asking around friends and relatives for help and contacts, it might be worth rethinking your strategy.

But how does a rusty stay-at-home mum get on the phone and make the employers of Britain sit up and listen? How do you reinvigorate your professional network when you left work so long ago and have hardly managed to keep up with friends, never mind distant work contacts? When the last time you looked your 'network' was a couple of phone numbers scribbled on the back of an envelope, blurred by coffee rings and competing for space with a splodge of tomato sauce? Or your carefully detailed contact numbers and personal details for all your professional contacts proves to be useless because you have decided to move to a completely different area of work?

Networking

Networking is a powerful job-seeking tool. Estimates of the number of people who find work through friends, family or company contacts vary from 30 per cent up to 70 per cent.

I would say that across the job market as a whole, at least 70 per cent of all jobs are filled by organizations directly, i.e. not in any way through a recruitment agency. This statistic is mostly anecdotal but based upon extensive discussion with candidates about how they have found their most recent employment. The most important thing any woman returning to work can do is to talk to everyone she knows about whether or not there is something in the organizations they have worked for that might suit her skills. This list should start with previous employers and then extend to recruitment agencies, her family, friends, neighbours, children's friends' parents, etc., etc.

Anne Wilkie, Recruitment Professional, Michael Page International

Nonetheless, many of us seem reluctant or feel unable to make it work for us. There's a sense that there is something inequitable or dishonest about networking.

Maybe we associate it with Masonic lodges and secret hand-shakes, old school ties or gentlemen's clubs: allegiances formed along class lines, loyalties based on who you know, success permitted and promoted for some groups at the expense of others. Networking has evolved into its own industry, something that we need to be taught. It can seem overwhelming, overengineered and something many of us are reluctant to pursue.

But hang on, isn't it what we do anyway – what women are especially good at? Cut through the jargon and isn't networking getting something done, or finding something out by casting a net over all the people you know, and the people they know, until the right name pops up with the right skill or information to get the job done.

Women are experts at it. It's what we do. We chat, we share information, we pass on names if we think they can help. We spread the word about great family doctors, good schools, plumbers and gynaecologists with warm hands. Do you know of a good babysitter? What is the teacher like in Year 7? Who did you use to sell your house? What is the name of your divorce lawyer? Do you know any available single men for my sister, my brother, myself? These are the questions we ask each other when we get together at the school gates, for coffee, wherever.

Is it such a great leap to, 'I am thinking of getting back into banking. Do you know anyone working in that field who might talk to me for 20 minutes?' or, 'Didn't you do a computer skills course recently? Do you recommend it?'

And this is largely what they mean when they talk about networking: using the rich and willing resource of the people around you – and the people around them – to help you get closer to your goal. It's not about asking friends if they can give you a job. It is about gathering information that will help you find a job. It can get you up to speed with your industry and help you to identify potential employers.

A playgroup or PTA committee can be as good a place to start as any. When Hilary Lauder was starting her online business – bubhub.com.au – and needed part-time staff, she didn't put an ad in the papers, she went straight to her mother and toddler group:

There were a couple of women having trouble working out how to get back to work – they felt there were no decent, flexible part-time jobs out there. That is exactly what we had to offer. I was a bit tentative, and talked generally about the fact we needed help, hoping someone would be interested – and one of them came straight up to me and said she was keen. She has been working with us ever since.

Nothing about networking is difficult. If you can manage a Christmas card list, you can manage your network. It's about writing lists, making phone calls, following up leads, having coffee and organizing the occasional meal in a restaurant if you like. If you can organize and communicate (and if you have children you are constantly organizing and communicating), you can network.

Sometimes it's fun – you fall into conversation with someone you genuinely find interesting, and networking is just an integral part of swapping anecdotes in the queue for the loo. Or it can be more formally structured.

Networking is also a two-way street. Not just because people you've approached for help and advice may well come to you for guidance at a later date, but because there may well be something more in it for them. It is common practice for companies to offer incentives to their staff to find suitable people to fill vacancies.

Real life

*I am just starting to put my own business together and starting off is
really tough – making yourself make the calls, putting yourself out of
your comfort zone. It has meant tapping into an ancient network –
people I knew ten or 15 years ago. I phone up and say, 'Can I take you
out to lunch and pick your brains?' I have been heartened by the
responses and it is really beginning to come to fruition. I've had some
good meetings and some good recommendations. I think if you had a
good working relationship in the past, if you got on well, then they'll
remember you. People like helping, I think – I like helping others and I
think if I feel like that, then others will too.*

Jacqui, psychologist and broadcaster, two children

Some companies have a 'nominate a friend scheme', with a gift
voucher or other reward for a staff member who nominates a successful job candidate.

Honey PR, founded by Louise Leadbetter, is a public relations
agency made up of a network of freelancers who come together to
pitch for jobs or make up teams to deliver on a project. 'We rely
on networking to know about other senior PR freelancers. All the
"honeys" have come to the network through word of mouth. They
are all top-flight PR execs and you know that they are only going
to refer other top flight PR people. So networking has its own
inherent vetting process. It is how we know we get the best possible people.'

Networking – what's stopping you?

I don't like asking favours from friends. That is what friends are
for. If a friend of yours needed help – a 20-minute chat about your
pet subject, or the phone number of an old school mate who
happens to be chair of a major television network – you would
expect her or him to come out and ask, wouldn't you? That is
what makes you friends. And if you couldn't help, you would find
someone who could. Favours are the fabric of friendship. If you do
favours for them, your friends will expect the opportunity to
return those favours from time to time. Let them!

I don't like asking favours from strangers. What strangers? There are no strangers, just friends of friends (and maybe friends of friends of friends …).

I don't like making calls to people I don't know. Hmm, this is not my strong point either – in fact, I spend most of my time engineering excuses to avoid making calls to people I don't know. But it has to be done, and it is not usually as painful as you think it is going to be. Prepare carefully. Let the person know who you are and how you got in touch with them. Be really clear about what you want from the call – it will be easier for them to help you if they understand what you want. Make yourself relax, and make yourself smile while you are talking – they won't see it, but they will hear it.

I don't think anyone I know will be useful. Suppose you want to be an astronaut but you don't know anyone who knows anyone who works for NASA. What do you do? Give up and go into real estate? I should think not. You don't know who you know, or how useful they may be, until you start letting people know that you need some help and the kind of help that you are after.

I don't know where to start. Successful networking is about having a plan and being organized. And the plan is the best place to start. List everyone you know, and everyone that they know. (Networking is as much about people you already know as it is about making new contacts.) Start talking to your friends and family about what you are trying to achieve. They may offer help.

Give yourself a structure. Create a schedule with realistic goals, such as the number of people you are going to contact each week (two meaningful conversations is superb progress, and better than 20 superficial, unprepared chats). Keep good records of where you are at: who you have talked to and what advice and further contacts they have given you. Follow up with a thank you – and let people know when you have landed your job. They will feel good about having helped you on your way, and of course you may be in a position to help them in the future.

I've called everyone I know, now I am stuck. Go back to your list, think it through again. Who did you miss out? Who did you call but couldn't get in touch with the first time around? Who have you already spoken to but should speak to again now that you have a clearer picture of what you are aiming for?

I feel really uncomfortable at formal networking events. The best advice is to take a friend. Standing at a Christmas cocktail party on your own, waiting for someone to come up and find you fascinating, is hard work. Arrange to go with someone. Even if they don't have a direct interest they can come along as a favour and you can do the same for them some time – but avoid the temptation of only talking to the person you came with.

Email experiment confirms six degrees of separation

In August 2003 *New Scientist* reported the results of an email experiment to test the 'Six Degrees of Separation' theory that everyone on earth is connected to anyone else by no more than six social ties – six friends and friends of friends. The success of the experiment suggests that our social networks are powerful and stretch further than we probably imagine:

More than 60,000 people from 166 different countries took part in the experiment. Participants were assigned one of 18 target people. They were asked to contact that person by sending emails to people they already knew and considered potentially 'closer' to the target. The targets were chosen at random and included a professor from America, an Australian policeman and a veterinarian from Norway. The researchers found that in most cases it took between five and seven emails to contact the target.

'Email experiment confirms six degrees of separation', 7 August 2003

The job ads

Open the job pages of any Saturday paper and a smorgasbord of opportunity unfolds before you – careers in all industries in locations near and far. From bold half-page ads for 'real jobs' at the big end of town, to one or two lines for niche positions in industries that you had never conceived of. A latte, a couple of hours and Saturday's job pages. You can be whoever you would like to be: a chef in a revolving restaurant, UN peacekeeper in Mali, a part-time telephone clairvoyant or chief economist with the World Bank – the lives! The opportunities! It's a fun, low risk way to while away the hours, but will browsing the classifieds and surfing the online employment databases get you any closer to finding a job?

Looking at advertised vacancies online or in the papers will probably get you work at some point. After all, the companies that advertise have paid to let people like you know that they are looking for staff, and you are available and looking for a job. If you can match a few other criteria you have to be in with a chance.

But the point isn't to find work, it's to find the right opportunity to suit your unique mix of skills and experience and deliver the right rewards and the flexibility you need.

Keeping an eye on advertised vacancies should be part of your plan – it shouldn't *be* your plan. Think of the classifieds, whether they come to you as daily email alerts or in the Saturday papers, as a research tool, a way of learning about the employment market. Where are the vacancies? Which industries? What skills and experience seem to be in demand? Can you get an idea about salary ranges or conditions from the ads?

Use online job databases to whet your appetite as you contemplate your transition back to work. But use them wisely.

> The online websites are making it too easy to apply for any job. Anyone who has saved their résumé with one of these databases can apply for any of the jobs that come up by flicking that button 'apply now'. We receive an inordinate number of applications, between two and four hundred sometimes – and most of them are inappropriate. We make decisions quickly – we have to, it's a flick of a button and your application is binned.
>
> Elizabeth Varley, Managing Director, Challenge Consulting

And have realistic expectations. Don't expect to receive acknowledgements of your application when you apply for a job from the classifieds, nor should you expect the selection process to be speedy. Companies which advertise online or in the papers will get a lot of applications. They won't necessarily reply to them all.

If you apply for a job that you are very interested in, follow up with a phone call and try to get feedback on your application. If you are unsuccessful, ask them to hold your CV for future vacan-cies.

Making the most of the classified ads

1 Look in specialized newspapers, industry journals, etc. for advertised positions rather than the one-size-fits-all weekend paper or a 'we've got 50,000 jobs on our database' website.

2 Ask yourself, are you *really* interested in applying for this job? Does it fit your criteria for the 'right opportunity'?

3 Work on your CV to show why you stand out as a candidate among the hundreds of others who have clicked the 'apply' button. Technology has made the process extremely efficient but thought, preparation and care are still vital.

4 If working locally is an important criterion for your 'right opportunity', look for jobs advertised in the local paper.

5 Make sure your CV reflects the kind of terms that might be used in a keyword search by the recruiter. More and more job applications get stored first and searched later, and don't go through a human filter for interpretation and selection.

> Just because a job is advertised online and you are applying online, it shouldn't be a batch process. All the old skills apply – about taking care and attention with your CV and covering letter. And each application must be unique. We can help by giving you a range of templates – but even these you should modify for each job.
>
> Michelle Brown, Monster.co.uk

Cold calling

Everyone hates it. It's a grubby business getting on the phone to ask people you don't know for something. Even the professionals – salespeople who cold call for a living – don't necessarily like doing it.

What makes us uncomfortable with calling companies cold and asking for a job? Fear of failure, fear of sounding like a fool?

And maybe a little self-effacement too: why would they be interested in me? These are busy people – why would they waste their valuable time on me?

But it can work. In fact an on-the-spot survey of 25 women found eight had found work at different times in their careers by calling companies cold. One was still working for the same company 30 years later, while another had moved internationally on the basis of a job offer she received from a company she had called cold. One day and two interviews after that call, the company took her out to dinner and offered her a job. She had until the end of the meal to make up her mind. She was with the same company for nine years.

In 1975 Nettie decided she wanted to get into the travel industry:

I had been out of paid work for more than 15 years – and I had an idea for starting upmarket small group tours to India and like areas. In the early Seventies there were few if any companies doing this. It was the era of hippies and mainly back-packers visited these places.

I did a travel agents' ticketing course then started to do some research. I found a company that I thought I would like to work with, phoned them and explained what I wanted to do and how I wanted to do it – and hey presto, after around one hour's interview I got what I wanted.

Thirty years later – and in her seventies – Nettie is still with the same company and still taking tours to exotic locations like Palestine, Europe, Iran, India, Nepal and Bhutan.

Cold calling certainly can work. Of course, not every call will land you a job, but if you know what you are after and you target your companies carefully it can be a sound strategy.

Think about it from the company's perspective.

By coming to them, you are saving them expensive advertising and recruitment fees and valuable time, and if you are the right person for the job you are improving their business. Every business has tasks to get done and problems to solve – whether it is drilling for oil, getting planes into the air or selling software to lingerie firms. And it's a competitive market. They need to stay

Real life

It's horrible to do, but if you start off with the list in reverse order (all the places you don't really want to work) and work towards all the places you do, you are well practised by the time you get to your real targets!

When I moved to a new town and didn't have much of a network, I got plenty of contract work that way – work as a drama tutor in a youth detention centre, tutoring at the youth arts workshop – and from that, work as an actor in the local theatre company – and from that I ended up top in the pile for the box office at the Entertainment Centre.

Hania, arts administrator, three children

ahead of their competitors – with innovative ideas, skilled workers, knowledge, experience, commitment and motivation: human capital. Human capital? That's you.

Even the most desirable places to work have staff turnover – people leave, even if it is not until they die – and firms expand.

Do you think that a business manager is going to think it is a problem to get a call from someone with an interest in their business – someone who has done their research and who is keen enough to work for them that they call to find out how their qualifications, skills and experience might be of use?

Recruitment agencies may charge the company between 10 per cent and 35 per cent of your first year's salary – plus costs in some cases. If they can get the employees they need without going through recruiters, companies will.

The mechanics of cold calling

1 Make a list of companies you would like to work for, and work through it *in reverse order*. That way by the time you are calling companies you are really keen on, you will have had some practice.

2 Do some research. Know why you are interested in a particular company and what you have to offer them. What are their business goals, what particular issues might they be facing at the moment, and how might you fit into that?

3   Write a short script – who you are and why you're calling. Practise it.

4   Do something that makes you feel confident when you are making your call. If you feel good, you'll sound positive. One woman did all her cold calling on a pair of roller skates skating around in her living room. 'I felt ridiculous, but it really worked.'

5   It's especially useful if you are new to a city or country and you don't have a network.

6   Try to talk to the person who will be making the hiring decisions, not the assistant. Try just outside of office hours – before 9am, after 5pm or during lunchtime – to catch the person you would like to talk to. Do not leave messages.

7   Know what you want from the call, ideally an interview of course but a referral is useful too.

Cold calling – what the employers say works

1   Yes, call. If you come to us you are saving us time and money trying to find you.

2   Before you call, do your research so you are not wasting your time or ours. If you can be clear about what you are after, we will know whether or not we can help you.

3   If we ask you to send in your CV, do. It is not a put off. Many companies do keep them on file and do refer to them when vacancies come up.

4   Present yourself as part of the solution.

5   Emailed CVs are fine unless the company specifically says otherwise.

The job agencies

On the one hand, there are tens of thousands of women who come back on to the job market every year after a career break. They have experience and a whole spectrum of skills and qualifications. As a group they are recognized to be focused, committed and goal oriented.

A survey conducted in late 2005 by the Recruitment and Employment Confederation found that 75 per cent of recruiters had been asked at one time or another not to present candidates who were either pregnant or likely to have children. Almost a third of the agents said that this was the attitude of a good proportion of employers – although only 12 per cent said they had actually acted on the instruction and discriminated in this way.

More than 40 per cent of the recruitment agents involved in the survey said that they saw no improvement in this attitude towards women of childbearing age.

On the other hand, there are businesses, big and small, looking for experienced people with a whole range of skills and qualifications, who are committed, goal oriented and focused on achieving key deliverables. Employers are looking for flexible workers to keep their overheads down and because flexible contracts can be structured to cover the peaks in business activity: hours of the day, days of the week or weeks of the year.

You'd think there would be a business opportunity here to bring the two together: a nice little corner of the market for a couple of niche recruitment agencies to sit in – or for one of the big recruitment agencies to consider. Both sides of the equation need someone to bring them together. The candidate needs an agency that will invest a little time in her, helping her to see past her career gap to the very real market value of her experience and qualifications, one that can reinterpret what the candidate brings to the table in terms of current demand in today's employment market and that can provide the focus, the network and the support as she navigates her way back into a career.

But they barely exist. Aspects of the service can be found, such as flexible work noticeboards, industry groups that run seminars and courses. And there are career coaches who help job hunters to shape their CVs and articulate their career ambitions.

But career coaches focus on the job candidate and they don't necessarily have the network among employers that the recruitment agents offer. The recruitment agent, meanwhile, focuses firmly on the employer. They don't have the time or the incentive to nurture talent or coach candidates about career choices. Women returning to work after a career break fall between two stools.

Nonetheless, recruitment agencies should be included as part of the job-hunt plan.

What do they offer?

They know who is hiring, in what areas, and what specific skills the market is looking for. They know where there are skills shortages or oversupply. They can read a CV in a matter of seconds and have direct access to employers at all levels of an organization and across the whole spectrum of their industry sector. They are a rich vein of valuable information and contacts.

On the downside, they work for the employer – not for the candidate. They are interested in you in so far as they can sell you to one of their clients. That is how their business works. How much time they are prepared to spend with you will depend largely on how marketable they determine your skills to be in terms of current vacancies and areas of demand.

If you are struggling to articulate your career direction or to crystallize your experience in terms of a specific job title or area of interest, they will rarely stop and do it for you. That is not their brief. The executive recruitment end of the market handles fewer clients and makes fewer placements each year, so they may have time to spend with the right candidate – but the gatekeeper process in place to weed out who they consider to be candidates with or without potential is more rigorous.

Register with them, but have realistic expectations of what they can offer. Let them know who you are and what you excel in, and what you are looking for, but don't expect them to take your details and start phoning around on your behalf. What's in it for them?

Wherever you can get in to see a recruitment consultant, do so. Talk to them and get feedback on the market and on how they feel your CV may or may not resonate with employers.

Don't ignore the niche agencies. They have often built their business on a few very close relationships with employers and know them inside out. If those employers are in your target

I look at every résumé that is sent in but I see very few people from the basket of those that arrive – maybe one in eight. I am not paid to find jobs for people, but to find people for jobs, and I just don't have the time to meet everyone face to face unless [the meeting] is client related or [the applicant] is in our clear sweet spot in terms of knowing talent. Instead, outside of short-term client work I tend to map out those who I haven't met but want to meet and call them up directly and get them on our radar screen. This, I have found, is a very good use of my time in terms of tracking key talent we don't know yet.

Jane Allen, Global Executive Search Consultants, Egon Zehnder International

group, getting close to the agent could be an effective way of finding your way in. But don't expect them to do the legwork for you.

If you still need help with finding the right direction after reading Chapter 1, you may consider trying a career consultant/coach rather than a recruitment agency.

5

Putting your CV together and preparing for the interview

You've worked out what you want from your working life now that you are a mother and you have a good idea of the kind of job that you are after. As soon as the right opportunity comes up, you need to be ready to sell yourself.

Gulp! Putting yourself on to the open market for the highest bidder – or for any bidder – may not be how you were hoping things would take shape, but when it comes to getting a job, that is exactly how it works. It is, after all, a job *market*. There are buyers, and you are there to sell your skills and experience. You want the right buyer, for the right opportunity and you should aim for the best possible price.

There are three stages to this:

1 Getting your CV right.

2 Knocking them dead at the interview (at least coming across as more or less convincing).

3 Following up and closing the deal.

Getting your CV right

Your CV is your most important sales tool. It is worth spending time on and getting right. Digging out an old version and adding a couple of recent jobs or training courses is *not* going to be enough. (No, not even if you print it on fancy paper in a trendy typeface.)

Your CV is not about you

The absolutely number one, most important thing to remember about your CV, above all else, is that it is not about you. We all make the mistake of thinking that the person who picks it up is interested in finding out about who *we* are and what *we* have done. They're not. A prospective employer is interested in his or her business – *its* problems, *its* issues and *its* opportunities. There is only one thing that they want to know about you: '*What can you do for me?*'

Even before online applications made applying for jobs as easy as clicking *apply-now, attach-CV* and *send,* you were lucky if your CV got more than a cursory ten- or 15-second scan in the first cull of the selection process. Now that job ads which once attracted 20 applicants can attract several hundred, a 'cursory scan' has become a 'mere glance' – five seconds they tell us – and that is if it gets the benefit of a human eye at all. Automated keyword searches of CVs loaded into a database are becoming more common. (That's right, you may be rejected by a machine.)

Getting your CV right means putting together a document which will be compelling in five seconds or less – yet substantial and enticing when subjected to more in-depth scrutiny at interview stage. It means letting the employer see *immediately* that what you have to offer is *relevant* to his or her business. Make it easy for them. They are not going to read between the lines.

There are plenty of places to go for advice and opinions on writing effective CVs. Key 'CV' or 'résumé' into any search engine and you'll find many thousands of pages of information – what to do, what not to do and how to do it, from career gurus, recruitment agencies, government agencies, HR managers, employers, journalists and advertisers. It is quite overwhelming. There are also scores of books on the subject.

Of course, it is worth reading around the subject from reliable sources, but the best advice on how much white space to use, whether to include the Saturday job when you were 16, wording, typefaces and whether or not to attach a photo, is only useful once you have a fundamental understanding of what your CV is *for* – who's going to read it and what they'll be looking for when they do. The rest is largely common sense.

Who is going to read your CV?

Your CV is a sales tool, and its job is to catch the eye of your buyer
– the person in a position to give you the job that you want. Don't
start writing your CV until you know what kind of job you are
after (see Chapter 3) and who is likely to be in a position to give
you that job. That is the person you are writing your CV for.

Understand what they want to see – and give it to them

When that person reads your CV, it has to be immediately clear to
him or her how you can make their (business) lives easier.

Companies employ new people when they are facing some
kind of challenge – maybe business is under pressure, there aren't
enough staff or they are changing what they do and need a different set of skills in the company. Whatever their issue, they are
looking for a solution. What do you know, or what have you done
before, that can be part of that solution? That is what they want
to see in your CV. You have five seconds or less.

Get to know the profile of the job you are aiming for

Build up a clear understanding of the job you are aiming for. Start
with the job ads, online and in the papers, even if you are not
ready to start applying for positions. Read the position descriptions and get to know what companies typically look for in the
role that interests you.

Use your network. Get your CV in front of people who work
in the industry and ask them how it stacks up next to the kind of
candidate they usually see. What are its strengths? Are there any
obvious gaps? What should you emphasize?

Describe your experience in their words

You only have five seconds to show the person reading your CV
that you have something to offer them. Use *their words* to talk
about your skills and experience.

If they want a candidate with 'business acumen', use 'business
acumen', not 'commercial ability' or 'business sense'; if they are

looking for someone with 'initiative', say you have initiative, not that you are a 'self starter' or like to 'work alone'. You may consider yourself to be 'customer service oriented', but if they are looking for someone who is 'client service focused', then give them that! (Provided, of course, in each case that you really have these skills.)

It might not be creative, but this is a time for pragmatism. Here are three reasons why:

1   If you've got it, flaunt it – in terms they recognize and can absorb in five seconds or less. Don't expect them to guess or read between the lines. With 299 other CVs to go through, they won't.

2   Industries, companies and even work teams have their own way of talking about the work they do. Industry jargon can be about workplace culture, processes, technologies and different priorities. *How* you talk can say a lot about what you have to say. No use claiming on your CV that you are up to date with emerging technologies if the words you use haven't been heard since the early 1990s.

3   Finally, and most pragmatic of all, if your CV goes on to a database, the company will use their own terms for the keyword search, not yours.

Every time you apply for a job or send your CV to a company on spec, make sure that you customize it to suit whatever you have been able to find out about the specific job and organization that you are targeting.

Remember, the golden rule of CV writing is that your CV isn't about you. It may list *your* work history and *your* qualifications, but it's about the company you want to work for and what you can do for them.

Use facts and examples

The person who reads your CV wants facts. Give them as many relevant facts to back up what you are saying as you can – while keeping an eye on the accepted maximum length of two A4 pages (three if you absolutely have to, but only if you have more than 15 years' experience).

Think numbers; they are easier to scan and to understand (remember, five seconds or less). So include sales figures, size of budget, number of staff, number of projects and so on.

> I don't want people telling me they are 'great leaders' or 'successful team players'. I'll make that call myself when I interview them. I want their CVs to tell me what kind of situation they were in that required leadership, and how they handled the situations. I want to know when they had to work in a team – and how that went.
>
> Jane Allen, Egon Zehnder International

What if you don't have what they are looking for?

If you write your CV thinking, 'Who is going to read this, and what will they want to see?', any gaps in your experience and skills will reveal themselves sooner than if your approach is, 'How can I squeeze my work history into two pages?' And the sooner the better, of course, because that gives you time to do something to fill the gaps:

- Take a short course to update you on common computer programs; try adult education centres, continuing education programmes or private colleges.
- If you need a college or university qualification, you can enrol and start the course. There are plenty of distance learning options these days if you can't commit to regular full-time or part-time study. You can put the course on your CV as a work-in-progress.
- Think about finding temporary or casual work, or doing voluntary work, to gain experience that you think you will need to land the job you are aiming for. See page 164 for information on volunteer organizations around the UK.

If, despite all your efforts, you decide that you can't legitimately make your CV tell a convincing story to your ideal employer, don't worry. You haven't failed. Maybe a bit of creative thinking around your career ambitions can help you see things in a more achievable light.

Felicity Coonan, a digital effects artist with Animal Logic and lecturer in film studies, has seen so many people drop their ambitions to be in the film industry because they can't see beyond actor-pro-ducer-director:

People decide they want to be in films, and they think 'producer, director or actor'. If they don't get the break, they give up, but the film industry needs all sorts of people, with hundreds of different types of skills – caterers, accountants, artists, lawyers, administrators, marketing people, wardrobe experts, sales staff. Skills from other industries are completely transferable.

Whatever you do, avoid exaggeration or lies at all costs. It may get you to interview stage, but if you can't look an interviewer in the eye and back up what you have written with some facts and solid relevant experience then it's likely they'll catch you out, and that is not going to look good. If you actually land a job based on knowledge or experience that you don't have, it will eventually become obvious – and even if it doesn't, you'll probably stress so much about being found out that it won't be worth your while.

How to present your CV

Your first consideration is the content of your CV – determined by who you are writing it for. The second consideration is presen-tation – how it should be structured and what it should look like.

The rule here is simple: make it easy to read and free of errors. An easy to read CV is:

1 Well structured – the content is arranged in a logical and appropriate order.
2 Clearly expressed – clear and concise.
3 Neatly laid out – the layout is used to support the content, not to compete with it.

Structure

Structure is about how you organize your information. Different structures emphasize different information, but the most important thing about structure is that you apply it consistently.

The most common way to structure a CV is to start with the most recent job and work backwards, role by role, company by company. (They call it the 'reverse chronological' CV.) It clearly shows your career progression, is easy to follow and is the format that most employers are used to seeing.

Less common, but worth considering, is the 'functional CV'. This approach ditches the job by job breakdown of your work history, or at least relegates it to the second page, and focuses on the list of skills that you have. The idea is to get the employer to see what you *can do* – your skills – rather than what you have done in the past.

Similar to the 'functional' CV and growing in popularity with employers is the 'competency based CV'. Like the functional CV, this ignores the list of jobs and dates and lists your experience and work history in terms of what you can do. The difference here is that the 'what you can dos' that you list start with those that the recruiter has identified as competencies required for the advertised job. If you are going to write a competency based CV, you start with the job advertised, and specifically group your experience according to the skills and knowledge that the ad is looking for. For each 'competence' listed, the idea is to identify two or three real examples from your past experience that demonstrate this competence.

Competency based recruitment has evolved because it is deemed to be both fair and effective when selecting job candidates. With the increasing complexity of discrimination law, employers need to be able to show that their recruitment process is not discriminatory. Competency based recruitment assesses a candidate's suitability for a job against the list of competencies required to perform the role. It is estimated that about half of the large corporations in the United States now use a competency based approach to recruitment – and its popularity is growing in the UK.

Enough of the HR talk – which is the best approach for you?

Without doubt, the reverse chronological CV is the most common, and because it is the most common, employers are used to reading it and are comfortable with it. Because it is familiar they are most likely to trust it. On the other hand, the current 'big thing' – at least in the human resources and recruitment industry – is the competency based approach. It turns your CV from a historical document to a pairing of your skills and experience with those required for the job you are after.

Which should you choose?

The answer is probably a mid-way approach. If you structure your CV listing either your skills or your competencies first, include an abbreviated version of your work history on the second page (reverse chronological) – then employers are getting the best of both worlds. They can see what you are good at and how you match their requirements, and they have the comfort of the familiar chronology of where you've worked, doing what and for how long. If you are returning to work with a career gap, that will be visible in this hybrid version – but it won't be on the front page, first item, and so it won't dominate your CV.

Self-confessed CV zealot, and author of *Brilliant CV*, Jim Bright recommends a hybrid of all three, combining the reverse chronological format of work history emphasizing achievements, *and* a section detailing specific competencies that match up with the job requirements.

This approach has been proven to be more successful than the others. We undertook a 10-year rigorous programme of research based on very large samples of recruiters and HR people across industries, countries, clients and genders and the results fully endorse this hybrid approach. Our research was based on behavioural experiments and observations and not just on opinions – because we found what recruiters and HR people *say they do* and what they *say they prefer* is not necessarily the same as what they end up shortlisting.

Jim Bright, *Brilliant CV* (Prentice Hall, 2005)

1. The chronological CV

A typical chronological CV will include the following sections:

Name and contact details – address, mobile, email, etc.

Career objective – optional, but if you include one make sure it is appealing to an employer and doesn't sound too self-interested.

Work experience – with job title, employer, dates and relevant achievements for each role, most recent first.

Training – put any training and any licences you may have relevant to the role you are looking for first.

Education – the most relevant first.

Professional memberships – professional organizations you belong to; also include community organizations that you are involved with (especially if you hold office).

Personal interests – optional, but if included, keep brief.

Personal data – such as citizenship details that may affect working visas, etc. Could also include languages you speak, special awards and so on. Avoid unnecessary information like the number of children and marital status.

Referees – you can name referees if you have cleared it with them first, or simply put 'on request'.

2. The functional CV

A functional CV may be divided into the following sections:

Name and contact details – address, mobile, email, etc.

Skills and achievements – your work experience broken down into relevant skills sets, including specific experience, achievements and relevant training in a field. (See page 104 for a more detailed example.) Can be further divided into 'special areas of expertise' and 'other areas of competence', or similar.

Education – most relevant first.

Employment record – a chronological list of employers, positions and held-at dates.

Education – the most relevant first.

Personal interests – optional, but if included, keep brief.

Personal data – such as citizenship details that may affect working visas, etc. Could also include languages you speak, professional associations you belong to, special awards and so on. Avoid unnecessary information like the number of children and marital status.

Referees – you can name referees if you have cleared it with them first, or simply put 'on request'.

Skills and achievements for a functional CV

Depending on the type of work you are after, some useful ways of classifying your skills and achievements are:

Sales and marketing	Writing, editing and communication skills	Supply chain management
Fundraising		Cost control
Software development	Project management	Specific equipment
Teaching and presenting	Planning and analysis	Customer liaison
Industry specific skills	Customer service	Business consultancy
Computer literacy	Data management	
Desktop publishing skills	Knowledge management	
	Financial management skills	

You should be able to list two or more specific achievements for any of the skills areas you are claiming to have.

3. The competency based CV

A competency based CV may be divided into the following sections:

Name and contact details – address, mobile, email, etc.

Competencies – start with those listed in the job ad or job description and add any other key competencies that you believe relevant. Illustrate each one with two or three real examples from your past experience – work life, personal life, study, etc.

Employment record – a chronological list of employers, positions and held-at dates.

Education – the most relevant first.

Personal interests – optional, but if included, keep brief.

Personal data – such as citizenship details that may affect working visas, etc. Could also include languages you speak, professional associations you belong to, special awards and so on.

Avoid unnecessary information like the number of children and marital status.

Referees – you can name referees if you have cleared it with them first, or simply put 'on request'.

> ### ► Typical competencies for a competency based CV
>
> If you decide to write a competency based CV, the best place to start is the list of competencies that appears in the job description advertised, adding other key competencies that you have which you consider relevant to the position. They may include:
>
> | | | |
> |---|---|---|
> | Arranging social events | Editing documents | Recording data |
> | Checking for accuracy | Leadership | Repairing equipment |
> | Data entry management | Operating equipment | Reviewing documents |
> | Coordinating events | Organizing people | Running meetings |
> | Communication skills | Managing difficult customers | Selling products |
> | Corresponding with customers | Persuading others | Serving the public |
> | Counselling people | Planning agendas | Speaking publicly |
> | Delegating responsibility | Preparing charts/diagrams | Speaking foreign languages |
> | Gathering information | Project management | Strategic thinking |
> | Drafting reports | Problem solving | Supervising staff |
> | | Promoting events | Teamwork |
> | | Protecting property | Time management |
> | | Raising funds | |

Wording

As one career guru puts it, 'there is no use trying to bore the employer into giving you a job'. Choose your words carefully. Be concise. Use dynamic language and industry terms but not jargon. Use action words and bullet points. Cut out personal pronouns, 'I', 'we', etc. Remember that you want to convey a clear impression of the relevant highlights of your career, not a complete personal history. You can flesh out the detail during the interview.

Be judicious about what you include and what you leave out. Your Saturday job when you were 16? If it proves you have skills relevant to the job you are after, then include it. If in doubt, ask yourself again, 'What does the reader want to know?'

Some useful CV words

Directed, led, managed, supervised, introduced, negotiated, renegotiated, improved, achieved, delivered, drove, generated, grew, increased, initiated, instituted, launched, organized, cut, decreased, reduced, slashed, accelerated, designed, created, developed, devised, formulated, established, implemented, performed, pioneered, planned, produced, engineered, re-engineered, restructured, saved, transformed, resolved, exceeded, championed, facilitated, consulted.

Layout and design

In most cases, simplicity is best. Here are some guidelines:

- Use two fonts at most – one for headings, the other for the text.
- Create decent margins all round.
- Keep it to two A4 pages (all right, three if you *have* to, but only if you have 15 years' experience or more).
- Use headings to separate sections clearly.
- Put your name and contact details upfront, other personal details at the end.
- Include contact details in small type in the footer on each page.
- Don't attach a photo.
- Printed copies should be on decent quality A4 paper.

Final checks

Remember, typos on CVs can kill your chances of an interview. When an employer is looking for ways of culling 400 CVs to a manageable ten, a spelling mistake can be the perfect excuse to toss yours on to the reject pile – especially if you claim 'attention to detail'.

Check and double check every time you update your CV or print out a fresh copy. Here's a proofreading checklist that might be helpful:

1　Are all the headings correct – spelling, font, type size?

2　Are all company names spelt correctly?

3　Are your contact details correct? *Double check* your phone number and email address.

4　Check the layout – does it print on A4? Is the break between page 1 and page 2 in the right place? Has a recent alteration affected the overall layout?

5　Check the footers – they should include your name and phone number.

6　Read all the content and check for spelling errors.

What about career gaps?

The most common concern for women putting together their CVs after a long career break is how to be honest about the lengthy gap since their last relevant job without completely putting off a prospective employer. Here are some thoughts:

1　You are not the only candidate out there with a career gap. There are 2.2 million working-age women at home with children. Most of them will go back to work at some point. In 2000, 430,000 women with career gaps got paid work. Employers have seen career gaps before. Do not emphasize the gap, but don't hide it. It is part of who you are and what you have to offer.

2　Narrow the gap – as soon as you start thinking about going back to work, do something that brings you up to date which you can include on your CV: take a refresher course, join a relevant industry association, do some voluntary work, get a temp job in the appropriate field, attend an industry conference or subscribe to relevant journals.

3　Rethink what you have been doing in your career break. Are you sure there is nothing work related that you have overlooked: accounts for the family business, school PTA work, contract work for an old employer?

4   Consider how you structure your CV – organizing your experience by function rather than in date order may be more effective (see pages 102–5).

Where to get help

Your network

You will benefit from getting other people involved when it comes to checking and evaluating your CV once you have put it together. The best feedback will be from people working in the industry you are looking for work in. Asking for help with your CV is a great networking technique. The kinds of questions you can usefully ask are:

● How does my experience stack up against industry norms?
● What particular strengths do I have that could be emphasized?
● What may look weak to a possible employer – and what can I do about it?
● What kind of companies may be looking for someone with my skills?
● Does it read well and make sense?

Professional CV writing services

These offer anything from keying in and laying out, to a full career advisory service. There are plenty of them and they are easy to find. Beware of good 'generalists' or great wordsmiths if they know little about the industry you are applying to. Keep control of the process and do not be railroaded. They may have seen more CVs than you, but if you have done your research and have a clear idea of what your target employer is looking for, insist that they take your advice on board.

CV building software

There are plenty of websites that offer CV-building software, and electronic templates you can download for free (for example, monster.co.uk) or for a fee. You may find them a useful starting point. Make sure it is a British product if you are looking for work in the UK – and one that doesn't convert your spelling to American English.

Writing your CV – what you need to get started

Before you start, dig out all the old documents you have related to different jobs you've had and any study you've done in the past:

- Old job descriptions.
- References people have written for you.
- Old CVs from past job hunts.
- Any documentation of your studies.
- Any old job applications you have filed away.

Also very useful are:

- Any recent CVs from friends or relatives, especially if they are in the same industry.
- Sample CVs from job search and careers sites.
- Job descriptions for the kind of job you are interested in.

You will also need a slab of uninterrupted time, a place to work and access to a computer.

Covering letters

Much has been made of the art of covering letters. It has got to be more simple than they make it out to be – and I reckon it is.

The biggest mistake is to think that writing a detailed covering letter will do instead of a customized CV. It won't. Your CV must be tailored to reflect the job you are applying for and appeal to the expectations of the person who will read it.

The second mistake is to assume that your carefully crafted covering letter will be read by anyone. Remember the five seconds or less the recruiter may have for your application? Or the fact that it might be read by a database?

Despite this, it is still a good idea to attach a covering letter with your application and include the following:

- The job you are applying for, with the reference number if there is one, and where you saw it advertised.

- A one- or two-sentence paragraph briefly describing why you are interested in the role – and showing some enthusiasm for the opportunity.

- Your contact details – these should be on your CV, of course, too. This should include all your contact details, not just your phone number, so that the recruiter can contact you however they want to.

If you are sending in your application by email, put the job title and any reference number in the Subject line. Use the body of the email for your covering note – but also include it as an attachment with your CV.

The interview

Like any phase of the job-hunting process, interviews have attracted a lot of study. Consequently, there is plenty of material available on how to make the most of your 20 minutes or so before a potential employer. There is a mountain of books published – but be warned! Books with titles like *101 really difficult and nasty questions you might possibly get asked at a job interview* or *Job interviews – the psychological approach* may be more likely to give you nightmares than steady your pre-interview nerves. The millions (literally) of web pages and printed pages of interview-day wisdom can be distilled into one sentence: 'Prepare well, look smart and stay calm.' After all, the interviewer has usually only got three main questions on their mind:

1   Can you do the job?

2 Will you fit in?

3 What makes you better than the other candidates?

Preparing for the interview is about making sure that you can answer these questions calmly and with confidence.

Answering the three main questions

1. Can you do the job?

This is the easiest question. You wouldn't have reached interview stage if the company wasn't pretty confident from your CV that you have the skills and experience they are looking for. They will use the interview to confirm that you are what you say you are.

2. Will you fit in?

Company culture *does* matter and employers want people who are going to reflect the kind of culture they favour – for better or worse. They are going to make a pretty quick judgement about this – in fact, some research says interviewers make up their minds about candidates within five minutes. The judgement will be based on how you behave and on how you look.

How you behave. The interviewer will look for clues about your work ethic, your attitude to colleagues and employers, and your general demeanour. Of course, your true personality will not reveal itself in such a short time. If you come across worn out (after a night up with sick children, or a fight about what your four-year-old is going to wear to pre-school), they aren't likely to give you the benefit of the doubt. There is no sympathy vote in a job interview. A good performance is important. Shake hands, look your interviewer in the eye, and smile, no matter how you feel.

Do your research and sound informed about the organization, its goals and its current business issues. (Not just whether it has an in-house crèche, flexible working hours and time off in the school holidays – but make sure you know all that too.)

How you look. Appearance matters, even if we pretend it doesn't (and wish it didn't when you find yourself at the school gate in your slippers and last night's make up), so make the effort to dress the part on the day of your interview. After all, would you leave your car to be fixed by someone dressed in a spotless double-breasted linen suit? She may be a great mechanic, but somehow you don't feel you know unless you see the oil on the overalls.

Dressing the part will make a difference to how they perceive you and – just as importantly – how you feel.

3. What makes you better than the other candidates?

You will stand out in the interviewer's mind if you have some-thing relevant to offer beyond your ability simply to do the job. Remember, the employer is very focused on his or her immediate business challenges. You need to show that you understand those challenges and are uniquely positioned to help the organization meet them. It may be specific skills or experience that you offer, or it may be an approach you take or an attitude you have, but remember the following:

- Speak the language of the business.
- Illustrate every point or claim you make with a specific example.
- Present yourself as a problem solver.
- Reflect the issues and concerns of the business in your responses.
- Show that you can grow with the organization – look deeper into the nature of the job description and anticipate its requirements, how it might evolve.

Preparing for the interview

First, sort out the home front

It is no good putting in all the effort to do your research and get your suit dry cleaned if you are going to sit in the interview and chew your nails about whether your children are all right. You have to be able to put all thoughts other than the interview out of your mind.

As soon as you have a date for the interview, book your babysitter. Don't put it off. It will slip your mind, and you'll be phoning around at the last minute in a panic (not a good start to your interview). And make sure you get someone you trust. This is not the day to test run a new nanny or babysitter.

Make sure you can hand the children over at least an hour before you have to leave, and that whoever is looking after the children takes them away – to the park, the pool, wherever – so you can get ready in a calm, quiet house and start focusing your mind on the job in hand. (DO NOT be tempted to use the peace and quiet to put on a load of washing, clean the bath or do anything else you never get a chance to do because your young children keep interrupting.)

Book the sitter for at least an hour longer than you think you will need. The interview may be delayed, or (if you are going really well) may go on longer than planned. You don't want to be flustered because you are concerned that the babysitter is going to drop the children at the police station and head off to their second job.

Research the organization

Thank goodness for the web! It is now so easy to find out about companies that there is very little excuse for not being extremely well informed when you turn up at an interview. Good background research will give you knowledge, confidence and fodder for questions to ask the interviewer when it is your turn:

1 Check out the company website. What are the organization's goals and its mission? What does it say about itself, and what words does it use? What are the buzz words and the topical issues? How does the role you are applying for fit into this bigger picture?

2 Check the media to find out what others are saying about this company. Search the internet or go to specific media outlets and relevant industry publications. Try the Where Women want to Work site, www.www2wk.com, for the inside track on many large companies from the point of view of women who have worked for them, and how they like to market themselves as women friendly employers.

3   Check out competitors' sites. How are they similar or different from the organization you are interested in? What are their issues?

4   Employ insider knowledge. Who do you know who knows someone, who is related to someone else who works in the company? Can you use any contacts to get an insider's perspective on the company's current business issues?

Revise your CV

What skills and experience do you have that relate to the 'must haves' and 'would be desirables' of the job description or ad? What have you done in the past that illustrates that you have these skills and competencies? Prepare specific examples, together with numbers to back these up wherever you can.

In the interview itself, you are most likely to be asked questions directly related to your previous experiences. They will be aiming to assess your specific skills, character and attitude. Examples of the type of question you may face include:

● Describe a time when you had to deal with a conflict in a team environment.

● Give an example of a particular problem that you have solved.

● Describe how you have successfully handled a dissatisfied customer.

● Tell me about a project you have managed from beginning to end.

● Describe a problem you have solved. What was your approach and what was the outcome?

Dealing with tricky questions and discrimination

What do you do if the interviewer seems more interested in whether or not you have, or are planning, a family than whether you can do the job? Whatever they say, whatever equal opportunities initiatives and legislation is developed, many employers – male and female – are fearful of women with children. They think we will put the children first, won't be able to work late and will sit at our desks watching the clock, unable to concentrate; that we will want time off during the school holidays, will want to shift to part-time work and will be on endless leave dealing with sick children or sick childminders. And then, we'll probably go and get pregnant again. When they see a woman of childbearing age (anywhere between the ages of 12 and 50 these days), many employers still see cost, disruption and inconvenience.

It is illegal to discriminate against a job applicant because they have family responsibilities. Nonetheless, it continues to happen. Women with young children face more barriers to getting a job than any other social group. Seventy-five per cent of recruiters say that client companies have asked them not to put forward pregnant women or women 'likely to become pregnant'. (What does that mean? Women who aren't careful with their contraception?) A fifth of recruiters say that this situation is getting worse, not better.

Job interviewers must treat all candidates the same. They are allowed to ask questions that relate to the job in terms of hours, overtime and possible travel if they are asking everyone the same questions and if the questions relate to whether or not you can do the job. Questions like, 'Do you have children?' 'What are your childcare arrangements?' 'Are you married?' 'How old are you?' can be discriminatory, especially if they are only asking you and not all candidates. It is impossible to present an exhaustive list, but as a guide interviewers should stick to questions that relate to whether or not you can do the job – and leave your personal circumstances out of it.

But just because certain questions are out of bounds, it doesn't mean (this is the real world after all) that recruiters don't have other ways of finding out what they'd like to know about your personal life, without asking direct questions. After all, they don't need to ask, 'Are you pre- or post-menopausal?' in order to make up in their own mind whether you are in childbearing years, ovulating like crazy and likely to drop twins or triplets at your first meeting with the boss.

There are visual clues that they may use to base their discriminatory assumptions on – a wedding ring, baby's sick on your collar, a large swelling on your tummy the shape of a watermelon. Or they might try some gentle probing questions. It happened to me.

The HR department of a global consultancy phoned me up a couple of days before a scheduled interview and 'sounded out' about whether I was 'free to travel', 'had no qualms about being away from home for a few nights at short notice', 'had no responsibilities that would tie me to being at home at a certain hour'. In five different ways they asked the same question: did I have children or was I planning children? I was lucky that the experience was over the phone and not in the middle of an interview where I might have been thrown by the nature and persistency of the questions. I can only guess that had I given any indication that I did have children, or that my children would need me at any stage during the working week, there would have been no need for an interview.

Those questions do come. So how do you deal with them without lying, and without being seen to be discourteous? After all, this is still a job interview.

I suggest a three-step approach:

1　First, steer the conversation firmly back to the job that is the subject of the interview.

2　If the line of questioning is persistent and making you feel uncomfortable, try: 'I don't understand what you would like to know. Can you be explicit?' (A kind of 'put up or shut up' approach.)

3　If the line of questioning continues, make it clear that it is making you uncomfortable and that you don't believe it is appropriate.

Remain calm. Keep up your smile and your professional demeanour. You may not walk away with the job, but you'll keep your integrity intact. In any case, who wants to work for a company that punishes you every day for being a parent? Research shows that those companies do not thrive. If you feel the interviewer is being discriminatory, and you want to take it further, a good place to start is the Equal Opportunities Commission Helpline on 0845 601 5901, or visit the website at www.eoc.org.uk.

Follow up

Some career gurus suggest that you follow up the interview with a thank you note to impress your good manners upon the employer and presumably to keep you in their minds. That feels like overkill on the finishing school etiquette to me. They have interviewed you, they enjoyed meeting you, now they are going to get on with making a decision. A thank you note isn't going to influence that decision – unless you are applying for a job in a finishing school, of course.

The time to follow up is if you are not successful. An interview where you don't get the job is a networking opportunity. Most interviewers will be happy to give feedback to a short-listed candidate. They may keep you in mind for a future position, or refer you somewhere else that might be useful. After all, if they took the time to interview you, they were impressed by your CV and see your potential.

Negotiating your terms

So they like you and they offer you a job. It's a company you want to work for and just the opportunity you were looking for. What do you do – accept the job offer?

No, not immediately. Before you thank them profusely, keel over in shock that anyone should want to pay you at all for working and just grab the offer and run, think about whether you should try negotiating a little.

There are some compelling reasons why:

1   Women earn less than men – 82 per cent less on an average hourly rate – but for low- and mid-qualified women that accumulates to almost a third less in earnings over a lifetime. It's called the gender gap.

2   Mothers earn less than men *and* less than women without children if you look at lifetime earnings. Women with few qualifications are hardest hit – dropping behind by nearly £300,000; with GCSE qualifications you will earn an average of £140,000 less. If you have a degree, the gap closes to

£19,000 less than women without children, £160,000 less than men. The 'mother gap'.

Gender gap + mother gap = women with children earn between £160,000 and £500,000 less than men with equivalent qualifications. Taxed for having a uterus. Taxed for using it.

3   All the time you are not working, you are not accruing pension contributions (unless you have a smart financial adviser, and some spare funds to invest on your own behalf). Women live longer than men, but they are falling short when it comes to saving for their retirement. A woman with average education and two children will be 21 per cent behind on her pension savings; if she has four children she will be as much as 69 per cent behind.

4   Salary negotiations for future jobs will be influenced by what you earn in your current job. If, for example, you are paid 10 per cent less than other candidates, the new employer might think you are a cheap deal and snap you up – but they might think that you are 10 per cent less valuable. We judge a book by its cover, and professionals by their pay cheque. It is not admirable, but you can't ignore it.

5   Company bonuses and future pay rises are often calculated as a percentage of your salary.

6   Fifty-two per cent of long-term partnerships end in divorce or separation. Women are still the financial losers after divorce – by an average of £150,000. That is a good few years' salary for most people after tax. By not negotiating fair and equal pay, we are not doing ourselves any favours.

It is not just mothers that undersell themselves – women across the board don't negotiate to the same extent as men. In a study by Carnegie Melon University, women graduates negotiating their starting salary for new jobs settled for an average of 7 per cent less than their male colleagues. Seven per cent has substantial impact in earnings over the years. And if you are going to interrupt your career to have children, and downsize while you bring them up, that gap is going to widen considerably.

Still, money is far from everything – and negotiating a better deal doesn't have to mean asking for more money. Look at your package – what is really valuable to you? A training allowance? Study leave? Assistance with childcare? A review after six months?

If the company is offering you a job, they are interested in buying the skills and experience you bring. Play it carefully, go with your instincts, but don't automatically accept what is offered without considering whether there might be scope for movement.

Here are some tips on negotiating:

1 Start negotiating when there is at least an agreement in principle – when you know for sure that they want you.

2 Research your worth. Understand what you have that they want, and what the going rate for those skills is.

3 Remind yourself of situations when you negotiate successfully – with your children, when buying a house, when you are asking for something on somebody else's behalf. You have the skills – use them.

4 Work out what you think they need, and keep those needs in your mind.

5 Think about the package, not just the salary. Everything is negotiable. It doesn't hurt to ask.

6 Start with the easy things and do some give and take to show you are reasonable and flexible.

7 Don't take the process too personally. You are doing a trade, not examining whether you are a good and worthy person. They want you to work for them. You are just working out the terms.

8 How you negotiate matters. Think collaborative not combative. This is not just about getting more for yourself, but about what the company is getting too. Present a *win–win* approach, as the jargonists would say.

9 Have a bottom line – some things will not be negotiable for you. Know what they are and be prepared to walk away if you don't get them. There is no point in getting a series of small concessions if the big things don't work.

10 Smile, remain friendly and professional – enjoy the process.

Negotiating up

You will probably receive the initial offer verbally, quite probably over the telephone. Don't start negotiating straight away. Take down the details of the offer and arrange to call back when you have an opportunity to consider them. A follow-up conversation, in which you choose to negotiate on your salary, might sound something like the following (although I doubt many of you are quite as long-winded as this example):

I was delighted to receive the job offer from AB Ltd. I enjoyed meeting you at the interview and I believe the role presents some exciting and stimulating challenges. I do have a couple of questions about the proposed terms and conditions that I would like to go over with you.

First, I understand you would require me to work overtime up to three times a month, is that right? How much notice am I likely to get of the need to work overtime, or is it at my discretion? *(Show you are willing, just needing more details.)*

Second, I understand there is an element of travel involved in the role. I am really looking forward to getting out of the office and meeting our clients. Can you give me more details of the travel – how often do you think I will be out of the office, will there be overnight stays required, how do you cost and reimburse travelling expenses? *(Show you are interested in the mechanics of the job.)*

Finally, I would like to understand whether there is any room for movement on the salary. While I realize there is a learning curve as a new hire to the company, I believe that the experience I bring from Company X and my proven skills in Y and Z as we discussed at the interview merit a higher starting salary. May I suggest …?

Once you have your figure on the table, you can suggest ways the company can improve on the offer if they are not prepared simply to increase your salary. For example, an agreed rise on successful completion of the trial period, by increasing the company pension contribution, by increasing the bonus element of your package, contributions to childcare costs, etc.

There is one way of avoiding the effort of putting together a CV – and the stress of the job interview – and that is if you go into business for yourself. Chapter 6 will look at the mechanics of starting your own business and the options for working freelance from home.

6

Starting out on your own – freelance or your own business

If you are thinking of reinventing your working life now that you are a mother, the chances are you'll ponder the possibility of working for yourself. Why not? No CV to write, no job interviews to sweat through. No glass ceiling to crack your head against – your own corporate ladder to climb at your own speed, in your designer suit or a pair of comfy slippers. If you work for yourself, who's going to know?

There are two starting points if you are thinking of working for yourself: going freelance or starting a 'proper' business. Freelancing means selling your services at an hourly rate, or project by project. A freelancer needs to create a business structure to operate efficiently in the tax system, but essentially a freelancer's operation is limited by the number of hours a week they are prepared to work.

Businesses – and business owners – come in all shapes and sizes. You don't have to be Alan Sugar to succeed, nor does your business have to be the size of Coca-Cola. It could be. You have as much capability to become the new Anita Roddick as the next person. The beauty about owning your own business is that you get to choose what it means to make a success of it: whether it is to earn a bit of money while the children are young and you want flexibility, or to lay the foundations of a bigger, longer-term venture.

If you take this path you certainly won't be alone. Nor will you necessarily have to work every hour of the day and night: there are nearly a million women-owned small businesses in Britain. They contribute £115 billion to the UK economy, and nearly half of women business owners work part time.

Ros Jay knows the ups and downs of both freelance working and small business ownership. She went from being a freelance writer to running a business, with her husband Richard Craze, when they set up White Ladder Press:

We were both working from home before we started the business and logistically everything has been very similar – same deadlines, same desks, same childminder. So setting up White Ladder hasn't really affected our work/life balance or our time with the children. It is just that we come up with the ideas for most of the books and publish, market and distribute them ourselves. We still live by the same rules – we shut the office door at night and don't get tempted to go back in. We split the school run and divide the childminding during the school holidays equally between us and the childminder. The biggest change has been since we converted an old garage into an office and moved out of our offices in the house. Before we worked at different ends of the house, now we work right next door to each other and can hear each other through the wall.

So, what are the main differences between being freelance and starting a business, and how do you get started?

Going freelance

The attractions of becoming a freelancer are clear. You sell your skills at an hourly rate which is almost certainly higher than you'd be paid as a salaried employee; you get to choose your hours, work from home and concentrate on the job in hand, completely bypassing office politics. In fact, you do what you did before, but you are paid more and you can claim tax deductions.

Most industries have a freelance market of some sort. Here are a few ideas to get you thinking: accountancy, architecture, beautician, catering, data entry or data management, editing, engineering, events organizing, graphic design, hairdressing, interior designing (or more fashionably 'house doctor'), ironing, party planning, public relations, secretarial/administration, researching, teaching and writing.

Freelancing can be seen to offer many of the freedoms of going into business for yourself, without the risks, especially if you plan just a bit of freelancing on the side to keep your hand in and a bit of extra cash in your pocket. But if you really want to make a success of being a freelancer the best advice is to treat the venture like a business, because that is exactly what it is. Set goals – how much work you want to do, how much money you need to earn – plan it, cost it, stay on top of the paperwork, nurture your client base and keep your training up to date. For more information on what to think about when starting your own business, see page 134.

Starting out

The best source of help, as ever, is people who have done it before. Talk to other freelancers working in your field. Get an idea of how they have approached their freelancing, how they have set up their business, how they get clients and so on. People love to be asked to share their expertise – and freelancing can be a lonely lot – so ask them out for a drink while you pick their brains.

Is freelancing for you?

Are you:

- Excellent at what you do?
- Self-motivated?
- Orderly and meticulous about account keeping?
- Reliable – you deliver what you promise?
- Adaptable to different bosses and different ways of working?
- Prepared to get out there and network to bring in business?
- Comfortable living without the security of a monthly pay cheque?
- Personable? Clients come back if you do a good job and if they like you (mind you, if you do a good job they will like you).

Real life

I went freelance before I had children. I was a book editor with a major scientific publishing house, and worked hard and long hours. It was my job to farm work out to the team of freelancers, and although I enjoyed what I was doing, I couldn't help but be envious of what I thought was the control they had over their life and their work – the freedom they had to live out of town, and of course, when it came to signing off the invoices they put in, I could see that good freelancers could earn as much or more than I was.

Going freelance lived up to what I hoped – it was such a relief not to have to commute every day, and I certainly made good money from the start. I think it helped that I had worked with so many freelancers, and I had a clear picture of what keeps business coming your way. The key is to work to a really high standard, consistently and to be reliable about deadlines. If a client knows that you will do the job as well as if you worked for the company and that you will meet deadlines then they'll keep coming back to you.

What I hadn't prepared for was the need to market myself to other companies other than the one I had just left. It took about a year to build up a reputation with three or four major clients, but once that was established, work was fairly consistent. If you have a good relationship with a few key suppliers, then all the paperwork, invoicing, chasing payments, etc. becomes easier.

The downsides of freelancing include things like having the courage to refuse work – you are always tempted to take on more, because you never know when the next project may come – so giving yourself time off falls by the wayside a bit. And for me, after three years on my own, I was hankering to get back into an office environment, rebuild my contacts, update myself on what was going on in the industry, so I moved to an in-house job again for two years. Now that I have had my daughter, I am thinking of going back to freelance for the flexibility. I think the mix of freelance for a few years and working in-house for periods is a great balance for me.

Julie, book editor, one child

Setting up your business

There are a few different options for you to consider when you are setting yourself up to freelance. You can simply declare yourself to be self-employed (you must notify the tax office – call the Newly Self-Employed Helpline on 08459 154 515) and get going. Or you can give your business a more formal structure. Options include:

● Setting up as a limited company.

● Working through an umbrella company.

● Working through an agency.

Each option has different advantages which are best considered with reference to your particular situation, and with professional tax advice. This is a regulated area which has had some considerable scrutiny by the tax office to ensure that deductions claimed are reasonable, and that companies aren't defrauding the system by changing employees' status to freelance in order to avoid the costs of an employee. Furthermore, a professional will help you understand the right business structure for your purposes and how to maximize the tax advantages – one of the incentives of going freelance in the first place.

Finding work

If you have just had a baby and you plan to freelance part time as a way of keeping your hand in and earn some extra cash, the easiest place to start is the company you have just left. If they offer you work, be aware that under IR35 you cannot be seen to have too much of your work coming from one source – or HM Revenue and Customs will consider you a de facto employee of that company and will start to question your freelance status. So, early on in your freelancing career you will need to consider where else you can source work.

Networking

Yes, networking again (see page 80). The main channel for freelance work is without doubt word of mouth. People commissioning a job give it to someone whose work they have seen before or at least whose reputation precedes them. The first thing you need to do when you open your doors as a freelancer is to contact everyone you have ever worked for or with. Let them know you are now in the market for work. Ask for recommendations and referrals if there is no work immediately; also ask one or two to act as referees for new clients. Beyond your existing list of contacts, research the industry and target suitable companies – those you know use the kind of service you offer. Keep a list of your contacts and make it a rule to keep in touch every three or so months.

Directories and email lists

There are several online freelance registries you can sign up to. It doesn't hurt putting your name down on the ones that are free (although you risk being put on someone's mailing list). However, most industries have one or two leading registries that have particular credibility within the industry. Find out if one exists in your field and, if so, how you can be included on it. See page 130 for a list of websites which have directories you can join.

Industries have who's-who directories that list key people and their contact details – managing editors, television producers, art directors and so on. Knowing who to ask for is invaluable for freelancers calling companies cold for work. Find out what is the who's-who for your industry. Some examples include *The Freelance Photographer's Market Handbook*, the *Writers' and Artists' Yearbook*, *The Knowledge* (film production and TV), *Willings Press Guide*.

Agencies

One way to get work is to register with one or a number of agencies. The downside, of course, is that the agency will take a commission on every job. On the other hand, they will have a wider client base and may be a great fall back while you are building your own list of clients, or building up your portfolio of work. You can find agencies listed in the *Yellow Pages*, or ask around among other freelancers for recommendations. If your name is put to an agency by someone already on their books, this might help get a start with them.

How do you work out how much to charge?

First, this is a business, not a hobby. Work out what it costs you to do the work you are commissioned to do. Include a portion for overheads – lighting, heating, depreciation on your equipment, travel, plus direct costs: paper, post, packaging, couriers unless you can charge these back to your client. You need to decide what is an acceptable profit for you to make – one that covers the cost of your time. I always include a loading for childcare. It is not an official cost but if the profit on a job doesn't pay someone to look after the children, then I am losing money by working.

When you have worked out what it costs you, and what you need to earn on top of the costs to make it worth your while, compare your rates to what you can find out about the going market rates.

Find out what others are charging by asking around. You can also find published rates for some freelance work. The National Union of Journalists, for example, produces the *Freelance Fees Guide*. This lists freelance rates for a wide range of jobs from book editing, indexing and illustrating, to public relations work, photography and broadcast journalism. You can access it for free at www.londonfreelance.org.

Quote what you truly believe the job to be worth and be prepared to negotiate. Don't take on work at any cost, however. Have a bottom line figure that you will not go under. If your negotiations happen over the phone, follow up immediately in writing with the confirmed amount and any other important details about the job.

Accounts and paperwork – keeping up with the business side

Most people go freelance because they are competent writers, or illustrators, events organizers and so on. Few would claim to be talented accountants, but, as I have already said, as a freelancer you are running your own business and you are responsible for the paperwork. Keeping good records is key to keeping your accounts up to date, making the most of your tax deductions and basically keeping the cash flow in matching the flow out.

Set aside regular time every week to do paperwork – to invoice, chase payments, organize your receipts. It is so easy to focus on the bits of your work that you are paid to do, but it can cost you a lot of money if you don't keep up with the admin.

It is helpful if you have access to a good accountant, and keeping your own records in order will keep the accountant's time – and therefore cost – down.

► Helpful websites for information for freelancers

www.freelancers.net – for freelancers in multimedia industries. Includes freelancers' directory listing, jobs noticeboard. Has an email newsletter and jobs. Can help with domain names, online portfolios and email addresses.

www.freelanceuk.com – media, creative, marketing, PR. Has a directory. Has comprehensive freelance information about tax laws, networking, starting up your business, insurance, marketing, etc.

www.sfep.org.uk – website of the Society for Editors and Proofreaders (SfEP). Runs the course 'Going freelance and staying there'. Also produces a directory of members which freelancers can list in.

www.londonfreelance.org – National Union of Journalists' *Freelance Fees Guide*. A good starting point. This lists rates for a wide range of jobs, from book editing and illustrating, to PR, photography and broadcast journalism.

www.freelancecentre.com – offers a free directory listing. Categories include accountants, healthcare consultants, landscape architects and computer trainers.

www.smarterwork.com – provides a marketplace for freelancers in a variety of disciplines.

www.freelancersintheuk.co.uk – contains information and a freelance community. Also the opportunity to list yourself in their directory. Has jobs noticeboard and email alerts.

www.journalism.co.uk – has part of the site dedicated to freelancers. Lots of practical advice and help.

Tips for going freelance

- Get advice on how to manage the business side of your freelance work.
- Take networking seriously and make time to market your services to new clients.
- Put time aside regularly for the paperwork – chasing the money (invoices, unpaid accounts, etc.) and chasing clients (networking, marketing your skills).
- Get involved in relevant freelance communities, online or through industry organizations.
- Build a portfolio of jobs and skills as you go.
- Consider setting up a simple website listing your skills, samples of your work and giving your contact details.
- Consider opportunities to pool skills with other freelancers when bidding for work.
- Keep a diary of things you learn on each job – should you have quoted more time? Should you have had a penalty clause for late delivery from the client? Should you allow more time for a particularly complex type of task?
- Put aside a portion of your income to cover non-working periods – even your pension. As a freelancer there are no paid holidays or paid sick leave, unless you pay for them yourself.
- Keep abreast of industry developments, training opportunities, etc.

Honey PR is an emerging model for freelance businesses. Founder Louise Leadbetter describes how it works:

Honey PR is a virtual network of freelancer PR professionals. The idea is that we support freelancers by providing the admin systems they need, and giving them access to the kinds of facilities that they might get at one of the big PR agencies – access to media intelligence services, technical infrastructure such as intranets and dashboards to use to communicate with their clients. That way the client gets the benefits of working with a big company, at the cost of working with an individual, and the freelancer gets the freedom of being self-employed, but has access to some great resources – and is able to concentrate on what they do best – PR – rather than being bogged down with the paperwork. We also form teams to deliver on projects which are too big for one person, or to pitch to a client for a big piece of work. It's the independence of being a freelancer, without the isolation.

Setting up a home office

A big attraction to going freelance or running your own business is the idea that you can work from home and cut commuting to as long as it takes to navigate a path from the kitchen to the room you are going to work in, carrying a hot coffee and not tripping over toddlers or toddler toys. Working from home keeps overheads down and you can claim tax rebates on office expenses.

Here is a list of things to consider if you choose to set up an office at home.

Insurance

Check with your insurer that domestic insurance covers any work you will be doing at home, the equipment you will have in your office and any work related visitors that you have. There may be an increase in your existing premium but it won't necessarily mean you need to take out business insurance.

Occupational health and safety issues

Just because you are boss, union rep and employee rolled into one, it doesn't mean you should ignore basic health and safety procedures. Make sure your working environment is comfortable and not going to cause you strain or injury, that the lighting is good and that any computer and electrical equipment is installed safely with no dangerous leads to entangle you or the children. Take regular breaks during your working day (or night).

Council regulations

Check with your local authority that your business activities fit within planning restrictions. You may have to register your business activities – even if you are a small operation using the spare room as an office and have no employees. There is a range of planning rules, such as what notices you can and can't display outside of your house.

Tax

Make sure you know what expenses you are entitled to claim, and keep all receipts. There may be capital gains tax implications if you claim for part of your home expenses as business expenses. Check with the tax office or your accountant.

Boundaries

Create and enforce boundaries between your personal and working life. Know when you are 'at work' and when you are at home. Do not confuse emptying the dishwasher with making an important phone call, or weeding the lawn with writing a client report. Keep household paperwork separate – and somewhere you can't see it so you don't find yourself paying bills, etc. just because they are on your desk. Make sure your family understands your office space, and if and when they are allowed in it.

Childminding and other dependent care

You simply *cannot* work and look after children. Babies maybe (if they sleep a lot and before they can crawl). Other than that, if you are working with children in the house, you do need to have another adult there to supervise them. Be warned. Some childminders and nannies don't like looking after children when one of the parents is working from home, so it may take a little longer to find someone. Once you do, remember that they are there to care for the child and you are 'at work'. Helpful comments or popping in to 'help out' every time you hear a wimper will make the job more difficult for the childcare worker, and your child will take longer to settle to the new arrangement – leave them to it!

> **Real life**
>
> *Children adapt to what they have grown up with. If you are firm, they accept rules and adapt. My children have never been allowed into my office, so they never attempt to go through the door. They don't question it. It has always been out of bounds. The danger is if you keep changing the rules and let them come in sometimes, like when you are just checking your emails. You have to be tough with yourself. It is very tempting to say 'just this once' but don't break your own rules. You are doomed if you do that.*
>
> *It makes the most massive difference even if you have someone else looking after them, and you are not responsible for them, if you can't hear them screaming. As long as you can hear them, they impinge on you psychologically.*
>
> Roni, author and publisher, three children

Get your support networks in place

Identify professional organizations, online chat rooms or other people you know who work from home whom you can reach out to for advice or just company.

Stay fit

If you work at home, it is possible that the greatest distance you walk during a working day is from your desk to the fridge, to the kettle, and back again. When you give up a commute you give up the ten-minute walk to the bus or train each day – or at least from the car park to the office. Work out how much time you are saving by staying at home, and use a quarter of that time to exercise.

Starting your own business

There is no exam to sit, no job interview to get through before you are allowed to start your own business, but it doesn't mean that everyone is good at it, nor that it will suit everybody's lifestyle. If you are more than a bit haphazard with your household bills and managing your credit cards, do you think that you have the discipline to handle your customers' money and to manage your business affairs? How do you know whether you have got what it takes to make your business a success? And how can you test whether your business idea can be a viable business?

What do you want from your business?

A starting point for business success is knowing what *you* want out of your business – what will make it a 'success' in your terms. This may be money. Money probably is a large part of it, but not necessarily at any cost. You may be starting a business for the flexibility you believe it will give you, the challenges it will offer or the creative satisfaction.

Knowing why you are going into a business at the beginning will help you stay focused on what you want out of it – and not be distracted by what other people think it should be achieving for you. It will remind you to keep control of the business and its impact on your life. A clear goal for your business is a measure against which you can review opportunities and challenges that arise. Do they bring you closer or take you further from your goal?

Of course, you can change your goals. In fact, they'll naturally evolve as the business develops and your own needs change. But being clear about what you want out of the business will help you control and manage these changes so that the business continues to work for you.

What are you prepared to put into your business?

Being clear about what you want out of your business should be balanced with an understanding of what you are prepared to put into it. The two have to be compatible.

If you want to work two days a week from home, and avoid the hassle of taking on staff, conquering the international market will be more of a challenge – although not impossible, of course. If, on the other hand, your plan is to grow your business fast because it is financed by outside investors looking for a return on their investment, you are less likely to have control of your hours, at least initially.

What are your goals for your business?

- Financial goals

Create a steady income stream

Create a business to sell

Improve on the income you earned as an employee

Pay off short-term expenses (e.g. buy a dishwasher, pay off a loan)

Create employment for yourself until retirement

Earn enough to cover childcare more or less

Grow the business (nationally or taking on staff).

- Professional goals

Create new challenges

Make your own decisions

Keep skills current while focusing on family

Create a new skill set to offer to a future employer

Be able to set your own goals and rewards

Build a business and grow it

Realize an opportunity that you come across.

- Personal goals

Work flexible hours

Break through glass ceiling

Work from home

Have a break from the children

Realize a long-held dream

Keep skills fresh to smooth your transition back to work

Satisfy your desire for independence

Make lots of money and retire early, loaded.

Understand your goal, and what it will take to achieve it. Does it match with what you are prepared – or able – to put in? If so, you are on track to making your business a success.

If they don't match, can you adjust your goal, or be flexible about what you put in to achieve it? Can you, for example:

What are you bringing to the business?

- Business attributes

A knowledge of the market

A new product

Business skills and experience

A specific talent

Connections

Money to invest.

- Personal attributes

A willingness to take risks

The ability to make things happen

Drive

Ambition

Diligence

Leadership.

- Involve a partner to share the risks and work?
- Get external finance?
- Do a course or work in the field to bring you relevant experience?
- Reshape your goal to meet your current circumstances with a view to reviving it later?
- Put the idea on hold for a few months or years until you have more flexibility?

If you know what you want, understand clearly what it will take to get there and are prepared and able to do what is required, all you need is a killer business idea.

Good idea or good business idea

Good ideas for new businesses are easy to come by – they pop into and out of our heads all the time – although we may not always recognize them. Here are three good ideas:

1   When I am massively frustrated because the washing machine service engineer hasn't turned up or has but fitted the wrong part, and I am sick of hanging on the phone to their service department to whinge and whine when I have many more pressing, more rewarding things to be getting on with – I think what we need is a bureau for mediating customer complaints. For a set fee they could do all the chasing and complaining for me.

2   When you are looking for flexible work after having a baby, don't you think that an agency specializing in matching flexible workers with flexible work opportunities would make money?

3   How about biodegradable disposable nappies that are as absorbent and easy to use as normal disposables but which aren't wrecking the planet?

> Be realistic about your product that you are going to market with. Sit down at the table with family and friends and talk it through. Bounce your thoughts and ideas with them. They will come up with things you hadn't even thought of, and will be able to give an honest opinion of your plans.
>
> If possible, test your market before you invest. Local markets are a good place to start because you very quickly learn if the demand is there for what you'd like to sell.
>
> Believe in yourself and your product. If you don't believe in it, you won't get there.
>
> Be realistic of course – if you are realistic about what you want to do, and you have tested the market, you will find a way. It may take longer, it may take twice as long, it may not be exactly what you thought it would be, but you will seek and find the way to get there.
>
> Ivanka Belic, founder, Little Workers childrenswear

They are good ideas – but to make them *great business ideas* they need more. To see if the idea could be a great business idea, try answering these questions:

●   What am I selling?

- Who am I selling to?
- How am I going to do it?

What am I selling?

Most of us come up with a great idea for the 'what':

- My graphic design skills.
- A little light that flashes as you go out of the front door to tell you that you don't have your keys with you and are about to lock yourself out.
- A customer complaints bureau that takes on your gripes and mediates between you and washing machine service organizations, airlines and telephone companies, saving you the time and stress of hanging on the phone or being passed around with no resolution.

The more precisely you can define your 'what', the easier it will be to understand your 'who' and 'how'. Ask yourself some questions: is your 'what' going to be big or small, expensive or low cost, luxury and exclusive or no-frills? Is it going to come in a range of colours and materials, or one style fits all? Will it be a 24/7 'what' or just during business hours? Will you be selling just one 'what' or a range of different 'whats'? What other attributes might your 'what' have? Be as precise as you can. What you are selling will influence who you sell to and how you market it.

Who am I selling to?

Who is going to buy your 'what'? What do they look like and where do they live? How many of them are there? How will you find them? Do they congregate somewhere – in the real world or online – or are they likely to be on similar mailing lists, email groups or belong to the same clubs? What do they like or dislike? Do they know that they need your 'what', or will they have to learn how important it is to them? How are they getting by at the moment, without your 'what'?

The customers you identify will influence precisely what you sell, how much you can charge for it and how you deliver the service or product they are buying.

How am I going to do it?

What is the process? Will you need premises, an office, a manu-facturing facility, or a laptop and broadband internet connection? Will you need a sales force, a call centre, or an email address? Do you need to design or commission the product? Will you be importing from overseas? Will you get exclusive rights, or be com-peting with other suppliers? Is your distribution going to be online, through existing retailers, or by direct mail? Will you use existing business contacts, or need to strike up new ones – how will you do that? Will you need external funding, immediately or down the track? Do you know who to ask? Do you know *how* to ask?

The right questions to ask yourself as you work out 'how' depend on the kind of product you will be bringing to the market. Focus on the logistics – do you have an idea of what you are taking on, and is it realistically achievable given your resources and your goals for your business?

If you can put together your 'who', 'what' and 'how', then you have the core of your business strategy. You have moved from having a good idea to having a great business idea – and poten-tially a great business.

You have decided to go ahead – what next?

There is an array of red tape and regulation to become familiar with and gain control over when starting a business. This includes choosing a company name, registering a domain name, registering with Companies House, VAT, national insurance, health and safety regu-lations, local council regulations and so on. It can seem daunting, but if you break it down into small steps and decide what you are going to do yourself and where you need expert help, it will be more manageable:

We bought some accounting software so that we could automate the invoicing and the tax statements. But we thought we could save money by setting it all up ourselves. We struggled for about a year, and got it just about completely wrong, then we had to pay someone to sort it out. It took two years before everything was completely sorted.

Judy, three children

Put together your business plan

Start on the back of an envelope or a paper napkin in a pub if you prefer. What is your idea? What is it going to cost to set up? What is it going to cost to sell your idea? How many will you be able to sell?

Choose a business name

There are rules about business names – it can't be offensive or similar to one already in use, particularly to a business trading in your area. You can search the Trade Mark Register online at www.patent.gov.uk. You will also want to check that your company name is not in use as a domain name. At some point you are likely to need an internet presence. Companies that register domain names usually allow you to do a search to check whether the domain name you are thinking of has already been taken. This costs nothing and is easy to do. Type 'register domain name' into your favourite search engine.

Register your company

Limited companies must register with Companies House. To be incorporated (to officially exist as a company), you will need to give them the details of your constitution, details of directors, company secretary and any members, a business address and £20. They will then issue you with a certificate of incorporation. You'll find all the information you need at www.companies-house.gov.uk.

Open a bank account

Different banks offer different services and have different fee structures. Some have special teams who deal with business accounts and offer small business banking services. It is helpful to have an understanding bank to support you through your business development phase. Check their rates, cross-check their terms. Can you negotiate any conditions? When you choose your account, consider what kind of business you will be doing – if you expect a lot of transactions then an account with a fixed fee might suit you better than an account with a fee per transaction. Some accounts allow free direct debits or standing orders. Remember, banks are in the business to make money.

VAT

Once your business turnover reaches £60,000 in a 12-month period you will have to register for value-added tax (VAT). This means that whenever you buy or sell anything in the course of your business you will have to pay VAT. Certain types of businesses are VAT exempt, and any business can register for VAT if they choose. Full details are available at http://customs.hmrc.gov.uk, or talk to your accountant.

Find out and apply for appropriate licences

Everything from gathering seaweed to selling second hand furniture has a licence or code of practice. You will need to find out what covers your area of operation. You can identify what kind of regulations, licences and codes of practice govern your industry sector at www.businesslink.gov.uk, or call Business Link on 0845 600 9 006.

Getting the help you need to start a business

Government schemes and financial support

There is a government maintained directory of grants and other financial support you can apply for when starting and developing a business. This is called the Grants and Support Directory (GSD) and can be searched at www.businesslink.gov.uk. The database contains schemes from central and local government as well as private organizations – under a variety of categories such as support for internet based businesses, support for developing new inventions, support for women in business. There are grants for innovation, for export, for research and development. There are grants to encourage small businesses in particular industries –

Real life

With three young children and a husband out of the country for more than six months each year, you'd think that Caroline would be hard pressed just keeping track of what day of the week it is. But she runs a small business renting holiday cottages, as well as freelancing one day a week for a national newspaper:

We have two cottages on the west coast of Scotland that we rent out. It was a challenge getting them painted, furnished and fitted out. First, that costs money so we had to organize our finances. Then there were the logistics of getting it done. I remember long car trips up to Scotland with the girls. We had to sleep on cardboard on the dusty floor before we had beds, and I did most of the painting while they were asleep. It was a combination of making the girls feel like it was all a big adventure and making sure I had plenty of books and DVDs to distract them with when they got fed up. It was hard work.

Once the places were set up, though, and we had organized someone to come in and clean between guests and keep a general eye on the place, it was just a question of marketing. With the internet, it became a matter of getting on to the right sites and search engines. I have done most of that online when the children are asleep. The internet has changed everything. It is so powerful. I didn't know anything about computers, but I have set up two websites which get us all the bookings we need. Within 12 months we were making a profit. I spend about five hours a week on the business now and a couple of times a year we go up to the cottages to do repairs, keep everything going, and have a bit of a holiday too. With my husband away so much, I couldn't do a regular office-hours job, but we did need to pay the mortgage. With the freelance work one day a week, it seems to be working well for us.

Caroline, journalist, three children

like tourism and agriculture – and to encourage new business in regional areas. There are grants to help grow businesses, accelerate businesses, assist with payroll tax rebates for trainees and grants to teach trade show skills.

The Department of Trade and Industry funds a number of Business Link centres around the country where you can get help with applying for financial support, or ask for advice on any aspect of setting up and running a business. To find your nearest Business Link centre, call 0845 600 9 006 (minicom 0845 606 2666).

Professional help

Accountants

Find a good accountant. Preferably one who is familiar with small business, and your industry sector too. A good accountant will help you set up, stay on track and save money on expensive and silly mistakes like fines from Companies House for filing the wrong returns at the wrong time.

A good accountant will advise on how to structure your business to your best advantage – limited company, sole trader, partnership and so on – and on your statutory reporting requirements as a registered business and, of course, offer tax advice and tax filing services. They can also help with your tax – PAYE, corporations tax, VAT and so on.

Personal recommendation is the most reliable way to select an accountant. Try your industry group, small business network – or ask around at playgroup. There were two at mine, both skilled, experienced and looking for just the part-time work I had to offer.

Solicitor

Solicitors are expensive, but if you are drawing up contracts yourself or signing contracts with other parties you will need legal advice. Going into business brings you into contact with a vast range of regulation – the trading laws, the rights and responsibilities of employing staff, intellectual property, to name a few. Again, find someone who comes recommended and understands the financial constraints of a small business. Discuss up front how you can work with the solicitor to keep costs down. Small items like photocopying, faxing and phoning can mount up when charged at the rates some legal service providers charge. Know the charging structure and do what you can yourself.

Your support networks

When you had your baby, you joined a mother and toddler group or similar. Why wouldn't you join a small business networking group when you decide to launch your own business? If you are going it alone you will take enormous comfort and support from having contact with other people who are facing the same challenges as you. Networking groups will be a source of help and advice, and even referrals for new business if you are lucky.

There is a huge range of options – your local chamber of commerce is a great place to start. Find where it is located on www.chamberonline.co.uk. Other options include industry associations, online forums, alumni organizations from your school, college or university, women's networking groups and so on. Joining your industry association will give you access to networking opportunities and contact with professionals in your field.

Another great option is getting involved in a mentorship programme – either through an organization such as The Prince's Trust (if you are under 30) or a women's networking organization, or by approaching somebody who has successfully run their own business and asking them to mentor you (you'd be surprised how many will say 'yes').

Tamara Monosoff, ex-White House bureaucrat turned stay-at-home mother, launched a clip that stops young children unravelling the loo paper, and either shoving it down the loo or leaving the bathroom draped in it. Having come up with the idea, she organized prototypes, manufacture and marketing, and her product has taken off. She has since launched mominventors.com which offers free advice on how to take your great invention from idea to the market. She also picks up and runs with ideas that inventors are happy to license to her. Tamara Monosoff owns the business; the inventors receive a royalty for the use of their idea. With 250,000 web hits a month, she seems to have found a market.

How about *not* getting a job? Not jobs

How about not getting a job at all – at least for a few years? Aren't we busy enough? There has to be an alternative to getting a job and climbing back into the rat race, or building your own business empire just to avoid the stress of tackling the job market. Have you thought about a 'not job'? Not jobs are all those activities that women who 'don't work' do – whether it is bringing in extra cash from party-plan selling or selling on online auctions, working unofficially in the family business or taking part in activities that create meaning and value, but not necessarily money: volunteer work, PTA committees, creative endeavours.

Housework and looking after children are not 'not jobs'. They *are* jobs. We all know women do most of these, although men are getting better. In fact they do double what their fathers were doing in the 1960s – and at the current rate of improvement, they will be doing half the housework by 2015. (Which is great news, as long as you don't want help with the washing *this* weekend.)

Quite often the answer to that question, 'But what do you *do* all day?' is a 'not job'. Yvette has a not job – several in fact – although she hasn't been back to work since the second of her three children was born five years ago.

I decided I wanted to spend as much time as I could with my children while they are small, and my husband comes from a culture which says men should earn the money and women should stay at home, so he is reluctant for me to get a job. He runs his own business, so much of what he earns goes straight back into that. We really miss my salary. So I take whatever opportunity I can to earn extra cash. I have done everything – from supply teaching to Tupperware parties. I've worked as a Nutrimetics rep, sold clothes party plan and minded other people's children. I've sat on consumer focus groups which they pay you cash or in products. I even went on a TV game show when I wanted to raise the £250 we needed for a dishwasher. Oh, and I do the books for his business – all the data entry and reconcile the bank statements for the VAT returns. But, as far as my husband is concerned, I don't work.

Making money without a 'real' job

The decision of when and whether or not to return to work is complex and intensely personal. It is certainly not necessarily the case that women who choose to stay at home longer are necessarily wealthier.

There are plenty of women who stay at home *despite* the financial cost, rather than because it is an easy option – although as you move up the income scale stay-at-home mothers become more common. But across the board, the financial penalty of becoming a stay-at-home mother is considerable. Loss of earnings range between £160,000 and £500,000 over a lifetime (depending on the woman's qualifications) – not including national insurance contributions – and not taking into account the average £155,000 each child will cost over the years until they reach 21.

Stay-at-home mothers have plenty of incentive to earn some extra cash if they get the opportunity. In fact, women are incredibly creative about how they turn their skills to making money around the baby's naps or school hours. The direct sales industry has grown into a business worth well over £2 billion a year, largely on the back of some women's desire to base themselves at home and work hours that suit the family first and the business second. And online auction sites such as eBay are a booming marketplace where breastfeeding mothers can list a few items for sale during the 4am feed. Talk about multi-tasking!

Earning money without getting a 'real' job doesn't necessarily mean working without paying tax. Everyone has a tax-free threshold (£4895 in 2006), and can earn a certain amount (£94 a week in 2006) before having to make national insurance contributions. These amounts change, so do check with your local tax office for the latest figures.

Women trying to make ends meet at home sometimes do operate in the informal economy – but is this always a bad thing? A report recently presented to the government recognizes that the informal economy is a 'major resource in areas where resources are in short supply' and is in fact the cornerstone of how many people cope. Women have always earned a few extra pounds by doing cleaning or babysitting other people's children. And women who are trying to contain the costs of working by paying a babysitter rather than the exorbitant costs of expensive childcare will often pay cash.

So, what are people doing?

Hosting foreign students

The English-language teaching industry in the UK is booming. Over a quarter of a million students come to study in Britain every year. Many of them see the opportunity to live with an English-speaking family, taste the cooking and absorb a typical British family dynamic – at eight in the morning when you can't find the car keys, school shoes or third child – as part of the broad cultural experience. In fact, if you throw in a bed for the night, they will actually pay for the privilege.

Many families find the opportunity to act as a host family to such students both financially worthwhile and a pleasant and expanding experience from their point of view.

There are plenty of organizations that match students with families. Some are independent, while some are based at the language schools where the students are enrolled. Signing up as a host family will involve a check that your property is appropriate – has the right kind of accommodation and is handy for public transport. Students usually require their own room, access to a bathroom, two meals a day and some interaction time with the family. Host family organizations will give you full details of the requirements and procedures.

Real life

Before I had children I had a career in the music industry and certainly planned to go back once the children reached school age. However, our third child has special needs so it's important that I am home. Since we had always expected to have two incomes, that's how we had budgeted, so being creative about bringing in extra money has been important.

One of the things we do is host language students. We go through an agency and I joined one that was recommended to us. They checked out the house: there are certain regulations that you have to comply with – fire escapes, having a gas certificate, etc. They also suggested I come up with a list of house rules for the students like when it's okay to use the bathroom, rules about washing, tidying and so on.

They stay anywhere between two weeks and three months. I give them breakfast and an evening meal every day. Most of them are at college all day. On the first day we take them down and show them how to use the tube. But most arrive very knowledgeable. They come armed with passport photos, maps, everything. At the weekends they are keen to get out and about. We sit down with them – they get Time Out *– and we help them plan. It's fun.*

Family dinner is at six. If they can't make it, I'll save theirs for later. Sometimes we all sit down and do the family thing. Other times, we're busy and we just get on with things that need to be done. It's all very normal.

I do their washing and change the sheets once a week. I don't tidy and tell them to keep their door shut to keep the children out.

We have had students from Japan mostly but also from China, Spain, France, Hungary. Some want to interact, some don't. I find the younger ones love playing with the children. And the children love the extra attention. My four year old says 'hello' and 'goodbye' in Japanese.

It has been a gift. The money has helped enormously. Five hundred pounds a month is a big lump of the housekeeping. It pays for the food shopping and a few things on top.

It's been a pleasure for us. I find it easy and definitely recommend it. It's a job you can do entirely to suit you.

Candace, three children

Setting up a market stall

Markets and car boot sales can be a great way to earn money – or if you have bigger plans, to test a new product in the market without the need for big overheads or complex contracts with shops. It's not as simple as 'turn up, set up and see what you can sell'. Research what markets there are in your area, what products sell well at which ones, and get your name down on the waiting list for a stall at the markets that you think will suit what you have to sell.

Car boot sales are easier to book into and give you a chance to get a little bit of experience. Book your car in, turn up with your goods in a few cardboard boxes (items grouped by price will make it easier for you) and see what kind of interest you get. Second-hand household items sell well this way, but you can also source new products wholesale and try them this way.

If you want to get more serious, local councils often run regular markets, and there are private markets in many towns that might offer particular type of goods – antique markets, craft markets, farmers' markets.

There are regulations to be aware of, of course – food labelling requirements and food preparation standards if you are selling food, for example. You may need to consider public liability insurance and registering your company name and for VAT (see Chapter 6).

The National Market Traders' Federation (www.nmtf.co.uk) offers practical tips and advice on market trading for stall holders.

Here are some tips for setting up a market stall:

- Queue for a casual stall on the morning of the market. Only take a permanent spot when you know your product is selling.

- Most markets rent stalls but some don't; you may have to buy one.

- Think of it as a business. Keep a business diary, note down what stall number you had, the rent and whether it was a good or bad spot.

- Think about how you present your stall. Look at what other stall holders are doing. You don't have to spend a lot of

Markets are great for mothers, first of all because the markets are often at the weekend – if you have a partner he can mind the children while you do the market and it can be time for you away from the family.

Taking children with you to the market can work too. There are certainly enough women who take a young baby along and set up a collapsible cot by the stall. Older children find markets fascinating. There is always something going on – and they can help out on the stall too.

But taking children to the markets can be hard work. It certainly helps if there are two of you. Children need to be looked after – they need someone to take them to the toilets, get them something to eat and so on. And, of course, they are going to see things they want. You have to be careful or you could spend your day's takings buying things for the children.

There is great camaraderie among stall holders and if you go to the craft markets there will be plenty of parents who are in a similar situation – or who remember what it is like – and you tend to get a lot of help.

My children learned from a very early age that if they helped out, they would get something for an agreed value at the end of the day. It got them involved in what I do, gave them a good work ethic and they had a fair reward.

Lynette Rayner, editor and publisher, *Markets and Fairs Magazine*

money. Cover the stall with a good cloth and present things up high as well as on the table.

- Carry a float for the day.
- Put prices on your display.

Online auctions

Using online auction sites to sell new and used goods for cash is the new best thing. Everyone is doing it – and a whole mythology has arisen to lure us to its untold riches, its inconceivable bar-

Real life

I started off just making clothes for my little girl – I am a trained graphic designer and have always loved sewing. I started making clothes for my dolls when I was about 11. I didn't want a job. I wanted a hobby and a little pocket money and had tried all sorts of things – like selling my art – but that wasn't making much at all. Then a friend suggested I make a dozen or so jumpsuits to take to her mothers' group and see if anyone was interested. They went really well, and I got two bookings for more parties from that first one, and then some more bookings and so on.

I still didn't want to work – what is the point of having a baby if you don't get some time that you can spend just with them, I always think. I kept it all small and worked when my daughter was asleep. When she started pre-school, that gave me a little more time, and things started to take off, so I got a babysitter one day a week. It was the babysitter's idea to take the clothes to one of the Sunday markets. She got a stall and it really worked.

I kept the business like that until my daughter was five and started school. Then I let it grow another stage by opening a store of our own – but we still do the markets.

Ivanka Belic, founder, Little Workers childrenswear

gains. The idea may have been conceived in America, but Britons do like to shop and we do *love* a bargain. Didn't somebody once say we're a nation of shopkeepers? Online auctions were made for us – to buy and sell, and to sell and sell again.

For busy women who want to turn their 'pre-loved' items into cash but aren't up to standing in the rain at the local car boot sale – or for those who want to launch a new business venture – it's a great alternative to staffing a drafty market stall, or going to the trouble of throwing a lingerie party. If you can shift your stock from the comfort of your living room, with the children asleep, half an eye on the PC and half an eye on the telly, it has got to be the non-working mother's dream.

So what are online auctions and how do you use them?

Essentially, online auction sites provide you with a shopfront to sell anything you have around your house – you can even, in fact, sell your house.

To start you need to register, which requires some sort of ID check. The biggest site verifies who you are using your credit card number. From that point you are free to list the items you wish to sell. It is a good idea to spend some time getting to know the site before you set up shop, so to speak. See how others describe their goods, what prices they start at, how they bundle their products, if they do, what they do about post and packaging and so on.

Different auction sites structure fees differently, but you are likely to encounter the following: listing fees (cost of putting something on the site – calculated according to value), valuation fees (calculated based on the final selling price) and transaction fees (if you trade through a secure payment system such as PayPal which offers you and the buyer some cover if the deal falls through). You can add postage and packing on top of the sale fee up front.

Auction sites also offer a range of other services that you can choose to buy, such as software tools to speed up listing for frequent sellers.

Here are some tips garnered from the experts:

- Think how you list your product – in what category, how you describe it – and include a decent photo (you'll need a digital camera for this).

- Successful online auction sellers are protective of their seller's reputation. Offer a returns policy, don't charge a mark up on the post and packaging, wrap things with care.

- If you are going into this as a business, be businesslike. Keep accounts, pay your tax if you earn more than the annual tax-free allowance, respect your customer.

- They say anything sells, but if you want to build a business, the philosophy of 'buy any old junk at a car boot sale and flog it to fools online' isn't going to get you far. You have to have something someone wants to buy, and you have to find a buyer. The internet increases your chances by putting you in front of millions, cheaply and fast, but there are no guarantees.

- Online auction houses offer you a space – they do not cover you for losses or guarantee the sales in any way. There is plenty of advice available on the sites from old hands – look at it, learn from it. It is easy to get ripped off in cyberspace if you don't follow a few sensible precautions.

Real life

I've been selling things on an online auction site for almost seven months now. We used to have a children's shop but we've closed it and I have all the stock to get rid of. So far we have sold around 600 items.

As a mother it is something you can do as and when the time allows – I've got four-month-old triplets and I find that I can sit on the auction site for a couple of hours a day and keep things going. Sometimes, when I am up in the night with the babies I list ten or 15 items for sale. It doesn't take long, if you are using templates. You just add the photos and fill in the gaps.

Because I have very young children, my time at the PC is like a break. I really enjoy it. I can get my brain working. I need to. It can get fluffy. I answered one customer's question by email three separate times. And on one trip to the post office to mail out sold items I was half way there before I realized I had left the parcels behind.

From a business point of view, however, I don't think I would do it if I didn't have the stock from our shop to shift. It is incredibly labour intensive. By the time you take the picture, load it up, organize the packing and posting, it is time consuming. I worked in retail and the mark up was at least 100 per cent and up to 300 per cent. You don't have the overheads of a shop, of course, and the tax situation is different, but you do have overheads. If I worked out my time, costs as well as the listing fees, valuation fees and the margin I am making, I certainly wouldn't be getting the minimum wage.

I think if you are selling things second hand – then you'd be pleased. Our neighbour cleared out his shed and sold loads of vintage motorbike parts. He would have got nothing for them at the local scrap yard.

Frances, three children

Buying and renovating property

We are obsessed with property – where it is, what it is worth and how much we can make by selling it. Turn on the television any evening and you will see that it is perfectly possible to stack untold amounts on to the value of your home with little more than a pot of paint, a hammer and a handful of nails ... and 42 trained builders, 12 landscape designers, a film crew, on-set caterers and a celebrity presenter.

Doing it, getting it right and making enough to cover your costs and justify the work and the stress (especially if you live in while you renovate) is not a game for amateurs. If you sell when property markets are rising, it might seem that a lick of paint and some colour-coordinated scatter cushions will add remarkable return on your investment – but it is largely market forces. If you sell when the markets are on a downturn, a makeover might get more people interested, but it doesn't mean they are going to pay over the odds.

A good understanding of the property market – knowing when to buy, where to buy, how much to pay in the first place and how much is the right amount to spend on sprucing your place up – is fundamental making money on property. Beyond that, good contacts in the building trade, a flair for design, good luck and good management will certainly help.

Start with what you are *allowed* to do, which means you need to understand your local council planning regulations. Then think what you can *afford* to do. Where is the money coming from – and what is your contingency for budget blow-outs? Speak to local estate agents before you start the work. What improvements would they like to see you make – in what order of priority? How do they read your local market?

Party-plan selling

The success of the party-plan sales industry is firmly rooted in the fact that it has recognized and understood the need for mothers to earn money around their children's timetables. The products that have traditionally done well in party-plan selling – cleaning products, plastic containers, make-up, underwear – are targeted at the same group. And the method of selling – getting people together at a 'party' – also recognizes that being at home alone with children can be isolating. It's great psychology and whatever you

Real life

I trained as an architect then worked for a couple of years in property until I had my first child. Since we had her we have done up and sold three properties and are now working on the fourth. One house we lived in while we were doing it up. That made it pretty hard work – but it reduces capital gains tax so it increases the return. We have done very well out of property – the last property we sold gave us a return on our capital of around 300 per cent after all the building costs were taken into account. I have a real passion for property. I deliberately sought out the estate agency experience so I could understand the market and combine that with my architecture skills and interest in interior design.

It is just the perfect occupation for me – it makes use of my studies and my experience and my passion. It is creative and it has provided us with very good financial returns. We get builders in to do major jobs, but we do a lot of the work ourselves – so they really are joint projects. And I have been able to do it all without getting childcare so the children have me around all the time.

If you are doing up your own home, there is no time pressure – if your child is sick you don't have to work, if she starts pre-school then you can work like crazy for a couple of months – it's the flexibility of doing it when you want to. Constant renovations can put pressure on a relationship, of course, especially because we do so much of it ourselves. But you get to live in the results of your work – and that is the most rewarding thing.

The rest of my time I look after my children, I wash, cook and clean – that is all fine – but you wake up the next day and it all starts again, more washing, cooking and cleaning. You don't have much to show for it. But if I take half an hour out to repair the plaster on a wall or paint a section of it, I can see the results of my efforts straight away. I don't get that sense of achievement from just being with the kids – and I need to do something else to satisfy my sense of self-worth.

Sasha, two children

personally think about its methods and its underlying assumptions (women are most interested in cleaning their homes and making themselves more attractive), the industry continues to thrive.

A new take on the party plan is hosting a party online. Simply sign in and hand over the email details of the people you would like to 'invite to your party'. The business does the rest. If any of your 'guests' buy, you get a gift. If they buy lots, you get a percentage.

Real life

I went back to work when my youngest started day care one day a week, and my daughter was in her first year at school. My prime motivation was money – but I also had to get out of the house. I had a four and a half year old and a three year old. I was going insane and needed something just for myself.

Before the children I had worked full time in a pharmacy but the hours weren't flexible enough. Since the children were born, I had been ironing and cleaning for about a year which wasn't great and didn't pay too much.

Then I was invited to a cosmetics party-plan party. It was a brand I had never heard of. I knew about Tupperware, of course, and I'd certainly heard what my father thought of that kind of selling. But to me it sounded flexible, lucrative and much more exciting than working in a shop or cleaning for a living.

I went along and expressed interest. A woman came over the very next day – and she made it sound like the answer to my dreams. I signed up immediately. My family all said what I knew they would say – 'don't do it', 'it'll be a disaster', 'it's a rip off' and so on – but the woman who had become my contact persuaded me to come to the meetings and see what I thought. I thought, 'Bugger it, I'll give it a go.'

It was a time when my confidence was at an all-time low: my sister had recently died of breast cancer, I had post-natal depression and had split with my husband. The weekly party-plan sales meetings were just what I needed. They were all about positive thinking. They had motivational speakers and all the motivational books you could name. It all made me feel so much better about myself – and of course the money was potentially good.

Once I got started, asking people to hold the parties was terrifying. Before I made the phone calls I had to get on my roller blades and skate around the house – if you sound upbeat on the phone, you are much more likely to get a positive response. That's what they tell you – and it certainly worked. It was actually very easy in the beginning. I made a lot of money in the first three months. I was out to prove to everyone that I could. It was a challenge and the rewards were fantastic. As you move through the steps you are always getting products and gifts and commission.

The goal is to have about three parties a week, but I averaged at about two. Three would have been considered full time. I estimate that each show entailed a total of six hours' work, which included ordering the product and delivering it to your customers. Each show would last about two hours – any more and people get bored. I was averaging about £100 in sales, with commission between 20 per cent and 45 per cent based on a range of factors.

Parties were generally at night and at weekends. There were also weekly meetings. It was flexible, but not completely child friendly, especially as a single parent. I did have to get babysitting. Luckily with three sisters you've always got a babysitter. I have incredible family support and wouldn't have done it without them – or at least I would have done it very differently.

And if ever the family wasn't available, I could ring around the other consultants. We were all in the business for the same reason: we needed to make money and we needed it to be flexible, so most of them had children, and we provided a back-up network for each other.

For a period I felt great – I felt I was going to take over the world, even though every time I had to do a show I felt sick I was so nervous. After the first three months I plateaued out. The challenge began to wear off. Once everyone was supporting me and once they realized how much money I was making I lost interest. I couldn't imagine going back into it now. Having to make the phone calls all the time, pushing people all the time. It just wasn't natural to me. My manager was different. She was a natural salesperson. She simply made people want to have parties. If you are a natural, it is fantastic. If not, if you find sales hard, then it is hard. After two years I knew it was something I couldn't do any more. And the decision to stop was a big relief.

Party-plan selling was a huge confidence boost just when I needed it. I know now that I can get up in front of people and talk. It had been *a lifelong fear. I can walk into a room full of strangers and talk if I need to. It was all about positive thinking. It made me realize what I wanted to do and gave me the confidence to give it a go. I am now studying alternative therapies to become a naturopath and working part time. It will take seven years but I absolutely love it.*

Carolyn, two children

Getting creative

Seana Smith, author of *Sydney for Under Fives* (Jane Curry Publishing, 2004), describes how she used her creativity and the experience of writing a book to open up new work opportunities.

Real life

I arrived in Australia from Scotland with my husband and a very active 18 month old. I wanted to know all the beaches, all the playgrounds, the playgroups, anything to keep him entertained. We started exploring Sydney together. I started asking around – I have always been a networker – and collecting stuff in a Filofax. I got a reputation for knowing what was available for children, people were always asking me and I kept thinking 'there must be a book in this'. There was a similar one in Edinburgh, which I had found useful, so I naturally looked for a Sydney equivalent.

I couldn't find one, and I knew it was a project I would love to do. I researched the publishers and put together a three-page pitch. The pitch was picked up by the first publisher, who asked for a sample chapter which I wrote and sent in. I do think that the fact that my pitch landed on the desk of a woman who was pregnant made a difference because it was relevant to her.

I signed the contract when I was seven and a half months pregnant with my second child, but didn't do much until he was three months old. When we were ready, I put together a plan and we set off around Sydney with a camera and a tape recorder.

I spent 20 to 25 hours a week working – it was a wonderful compromise because much of the time I didn't need to leave the children with a nanny or in day care so I didn't have to go through some of that guilt, and I really enjoyed the writing.

If I hadn't come up with the book project I wouldn't have worked – I certainly wasn't looking for work outside the home at the time. My husband works long hours in a job that takes him overseas a lot. With the children so young, I felt I couldn't really take a job. We didn't have much of a support network initially, very little back-up, and he was away so often.

But even though I felt like I couldn't get a job, I needed to do something. I had always wanted to write a book. And with the five years I took out of work for the children while they were young, I knew it would stand me in good stead and give my résumé credibility. I am very goal oriented and when you are at home it is so difficult to get that sense of achievement. But when you complete a project like the book there is an enormous satisfaction. Having the book on my CV really strengthened it. It has made it easier to approach new opportunities and to get in the door. I am teaching at university a couple of evenings a week and doing freelance writing from home. It is a great balance.

Working for your partner's business

Another 'not job' that women might find themselves in is the one that creeps up on them when their partner or another family member runs a small business, particularly if it is run from home. The kind of casual arrangement that starts with the woman answering the phone – since she is home with the children anyway – and then work-creep sets in. Answering the phone becomes scheduling appointments, having responsibility for the diary, doing the invoicing, chasing payments, balancing the books, liaising with the accountant, the bank, the tax office and creditors – in fact, pretty well running the business.

This can work well. It keeps overheads down and the business in the family. The woman can be productive during down time from the children, keep her business skills up to date and develop new ones, and the transition from being at home with the children to returning to paid work can be seamless.

Helping your partner out in his business may be a great short-term solution for both of you, but if the arrangement doesn't allow for the autonomy, professional development or commensurate financial reward, or if it is misaligned with your own career goals, it will put pressure on the business and on your relationship.

Judy's story

When my husband went into business for himself I started helping out where I could. First just casually, then up to two days a week.

Jack is not an easy boss – and he treated me like an employee – no, worse than an employee, he was rude to me all the time. The first six months were awful. I was doing my best but I'm not a trained bookkeeper. I am a great teacher, that is what I spent four years of my life training for. After six months or so, things settled down as I got to understand better what he wanted, and he learnt not to treat me as he had been. I took on more responsibility and having a clearer understanding of my role made things easier.

I get a salary – we agreed that up front. But because it's *me* doing the work – and he isn't paying a professional to do it – Jack doesn't see it as part of the business in the same way he sees other parts of the business – the parts he does. He won't spend money on training, for example.

I've said we have to spend money somewhere – either on childcare so I can help properly with the business, or on the bookkeeping so I can concentrate on the children. It is so difficult to get both right.

I tried taking the new baby into work – the first time she was only three weeks old – she vomited all over the office. The second time her nappy leaked and I didn't have a change of clothes. The third time, as we arrived there was trouble with a violent customer. I had another career which I was good at which gave me feedback and promotions and pay rises. When the children are a little older, I will go back to teaching.

Belinda's story

Justin needed someone to run the business side of his medical practice – the bills were never going out. We virtually lost two years worth of income. Sometimes his invoices were a year late. You can imagine how cross people would get.

I am naturally more organized and more business-minded. When I took over I didn't know much about computers, medical billing systems, health funds and so on. I have built up a huge range of contacts now.

I deal with all of Justin's accounting and have five other practitioners for whom I do billing and accounts, and produce monthly statements – just the cut and dried side of things. It has become a small business and fits my life perfectly.

Life is easier now. Both girls are at school and I almost feel guilty that I don't want to go back to work. I have a reasonable balance. I work about four hours each day. Get up, switch on the computer about 6.15, check emails, what deposits have been made into the various accounts, etc. I sort the mail, then do two hours' billing and following up on unpaid accounts.

From helping Justin out with the business side of his work, I have created an income for myself with the work I am doing for the other doctors. I am using my medical training up to a point, and am able to fit the work around my main priority – spending time with our daughters.

Volunteer work

Good volunteer organizations encourage their volunteers to recognize what they are good at and to use those skills in their volunteer work. The kind of work not-for-profit organizations generally do means they are used to giving positive feedback, and understand the value of nurturing talent, and encouraging people to contribute in any way they can. This means they can be great environments for women who are learning new skills or brushing up on old ones when they have been at home with the children for a couple of years. Volunteer work can also lead to paid work.

The UK has a well-developed volunteer infrastructure, including walk-in volunteer centres and web based volunteer

> Pick a cause that you really believe in and start at a local level (if it's a national charity), perhaps as a fundraiser, or help with publicity and then move up the organization. The only way to find out if you can be useful and rewarded is to get involved and find out how the organization works. It is relatively risk free and could lead to a big upside!
>
> Mary-Anne, volunteer with National Childbirth Trust, two children

information services. Volunteer organizations around the UK include:

In England, Volunteering England – www.volunteering.org.uk
In Scotland, Volunteer Development Scotland – www.vds.org.uk
In Wales, Wales Council for Voluntary Action – www.wcva.org.uk
In Northern Ireland, Development Agency for Volunteering in Northern Ireland – www.volunteering-ni.org

Other useful initiatives include:

www.do-it.org.uk – allows you to search for a vacancy within five miles of your postcode.
www.timebank.org.uk – you log your skills and you are sent a list of organizations that could do with your help.
www.v-word.org.uk – a volunteer organization aimed at volunteers over 55. (The 'v' stands for 'value', 'versatile', 'vivacious' and 'volunteer', not 'very old'.)

Vicki's story

I made the decision early on that I wasn't going to work until my children were all at school. By luck – and good management – I haven't had to. We don't have designer clothes or expensive holidays, but we can put food on the table, and I can be with the children.

But I *do* work – I do around 20 hours a week volunteer work. It is children driven. I have been involved in everything that they have done – from organizing the dinners and barbecues at the first mothers' group, to running the netball team and taking a role in keeping their pre-school open when it was threatened with closure.

I get involved when I see work that needs to be done – there is rarely an abundance of people ready to do it. I loved the pre-school that my children went to – but it had problems and was on the point of closing. I didn't want to have to send them anywhere else, and so I got involved in the committee to keep the school open. There weren't a lot of people putting their hands up – and there was a lot to do. Planning permission for the school was challenged in court; we had three teachers resign, leaving us with virtually no qualified staff. We came very close to shutting the doors. We had to go through all the legal and administrative hurdles of setting up a business, getting licensed, finding teachers and stopping parents from taking their children away because the school was on such shaky ground for a year or two.

Funnily enough, although I enjoy volunteer work, it can be much more stressful than paid work. It's harder to switch off. I can go to bed at night and lie there worrying through something for ages – like 'can we get another girl to join the netball team, then we can register it and get it into a league'. I'll wake up at two o'clock thinking about these things – then realize of course that I'm being a bit silly sometimes.

I have got so much out of my volunteer work – the friendships I have made have been lasting. It has given me a sense of achievement as well as being very educational. I have learnt a lot about running a company in setting up the pre-school and that has helped directly with my husband's business. Volunteer work has given me great experience and I know it will be useful when I come to tackling the world again.

My husband is very supportive – we share the same values. We want our children to see us volunteering – see that you can do something 'for nothing' and get a great deal out of it. If he wasn't happy with all the work I do for their schools, the netball team and so on, I wouldn't be able to do it. He runs his own business from home and that gives me some flexibility – mind you, he will sometimes say that if I put as much work into his business as I do into the schools we would be doing very well!

A checklist for volunteer work

Ask yourself:

- What do you want to get out of your volunteer work?
- What do you have to offer?
- How much time are you able to give?

Check that:

- The organization is a not-for-profit.
- The purpose of the organization matches your own values and beliefs.
- The organization carries volunteer insurance.
- Your role is clear and specific.
- The organization can provide you with written information about its purpose and activities.
- You are satisfied that the funds of the organization are expended in accordance with its mission.

Section 3

On the home front

Forget superwoman – get the help you need

Earlier chapters have looked at what it is like to be a working mother, and how to squeeze the most out of your working life now that you have children. The final few chapters of the book are about what it is like to be a woman who is a mother and who works – and how to get the best out of yourself and your family.

Keeping the home running smoothly and managing to perform effectively in a paid job requires planning and support, and no one does it effectively without help. If you don't have family available and willing to help out for nothing, it can take a fair whack out of the pay packet. And even the most organized and most supported working women have days when the whole delicately balanced pack of cards comes crashing down. Working women with dependent children or dependent elderly relatives perform minor miracles on a daily basis. Remember what they said about Ginger Rogers? That she did everything Fred Astaire did, backwards and in high heels. Well, the goals we set ourselves to achieve at work and at home and in our relationships are higher than they have ever been.

Let's get one thing clear in case there is any lingering doubt – superwoman does not exist and never has. *Superb women* are everywhere, of course – juggling careers and home lives. Their children are well adjusted, and they do their homework more or less on time and their clothes look like they've seen the flat side of the iron, at least occasionally. But these women aren't doing it all themselves, not the ones with tidy houses and children who make it to football training on time. More often than not, they are coordinating teams of family and paid support just to allow them to get out of the door each day.

Real life

I get to the trading floor every morning about 7.30. I am always the last and I am the only woman. The guys look up and say 'good morning' and ask how I am. It is always so calm and so quiet. They have absolutely no idea of the chaos I have just come from – scrambling around trying to get things together, to get myself ready and my son to the childminder. I sometimes wonder what they would say if I answered them honestly … I never do. I just smile, say 'fine' and get on with my day.

Anita, banking, one child

Carolyn, a single mother and student who also manages a part-time job, relies heavily on a family network as well as before- and after-school care:

As a single parent I am incredibly lucky to be living within driving distance of my three sisters and my mother – with a big family you've always got a babysitter. I have incredible family support and wouldn't have done what I have done without them. To pay for my fees to study as a naturopath, I clean the treatment rooms at the college. This means being at work for 6am one day a week. So my mother drives over to be at my place by 5.30am. She gets the children up, gives them breakfast and takes them to school. Who else could you ask to do this, but your mother?

Meredith works 12-hour days, with a two-hour commute to her job in the City of London on top of that. With two children and a partner who also works long hours, she needs a strong support network:

We have two nannies for the children and a 'wife' for ourselves. The nannies take care of the children – one has been with us the whole eight years and costs us a phenomenal amount to keep – but you don't stint once you have found good help, and as long as you can afford it. Our 'wife' takes care of us, runs all our errands, does the shopping, the cooking, the cleaning, the ironing. It means that when we are together at the weekend, every single waking moment is for the four of us – to snuggle in bed or climb trees, with no concerns about household chores.

You may not need two nannies and a 'wife' of course – a cleaner for a couple of hours once or twice a month might be all you need to create a sense of sanity and order around the home every now and then. Or it might be as simple as organizing a school pick-up and drop-off rota with a group of other parents.

Once you have accepted that you can't do it all yourself (no one else does), your next hurdle is getting the help you need. It's not quite as obvious as it sounds. The first step to getting help may mean letting go of some of those 'big rules' that you have set yourself as your way of measuring whether or not you are a good mother. (Like my persistent need to make sure every family birthday is celebrated with a home-made birthday cake. It is messy, time consuming and doesn't necessarily taste very good – yet it is a ritual I drag the children through several times a year. They only put up with it because they get to lick the spoon at the end. I can't describe their relief this year when, against all my rules for happy homemaking, we bought a mudcake instead of throwing together the usual home-made carrot cake, shaped to look like who-knows-what for their dad's birthday.)

If you are going to get the help you need, you first need to be honest with yourself about what you can and can't do. And you will need to delegate – not just a list of tasks you stick on the fridge each morning, but the responsibility for the organizing and the decision making and, not easily for some of us, letting go of some of the control.

How do you get the help you need?

Be honest with yourself that you need help. Without wanting to make it sound like a drug addiction (very few of us get a high from cleaning fluids or dust mites), some of us do cling like addicts to the belief that we should and can conquer this domestic goddess thing single handedly. It's not true.

Sources of help

The main sources of help are:

- Partner
- Family
- Community
- Paid help/childcare.

As you prepare to go back to work, be clear about your priorities. Make sure you have reasonable expectations of what you can achieve personally and what help you will need. Be especially clear with your family about what support you will require from them. Relationships will need to be renegotiated, priorities agreed and tasks redivided. You will be a rare family if you do not need paid support of some kind or other. Work out what is going to be the most effective way to spend the money you have budgeted for help, what government rebates might be available and how you can source the help.

It's not 'help, *any* help' that you need. It is specific help. Particular things need to be done, at particular times, to keep the wheels of everyone's life and work ticking over. So you need to be clear about what those tasks are – what *you* can still do, what *you* want to keep doing (bedtime stories, putting clothes out at night, reading practice perhaps) and where you need to share the load.

You might want to start with a long list of everything that needs to be done – lists headed 'children', 'the house', 'shopping', 'finances' and so on. Or you could try mapping out the week. Who is where, when, and what needs to be done to get them there. Whatever works best for you, the important thing is to involve your partner/the children's father from the very beginning. Not only will he think of things that you haven't, but if you map out everything together, you share a complete picture of what you are facing from the start. It will be much easier then for him to under-stand the importance of doing his bit – or to appreciate why all the family's holiday money has been blown on babysitting and cleaning. It also gives you a chance to agree on what is and isn't important – and maybe agree to knock a few chores off the list for a year or two – or perhaps until your baby is old enough to do them for you.

When you have got your list, you can start dividing things up – plan what you can do between you and what other help you might need to fill the gaps. Other help can be the children, if they are old enough, friends, neighbours, family and, of course, paid childcare and help around the house (see page 183).

This all sounds like domestic bliss. Two reasonable adults sit down and talk in a mature way about how to manage their joint responsibilities for housework and childcare. Let's get real. Who does what around the house and whether they do it in the right way causes more disputes than just about anything. And despite the fact that women have been banging on about it loudly since the 1960s (apparently everyone was in perfectly balanced domestic bliss in the 1950s), it remains an issue in most households.

The media discussion of work/life balance focuses on the external stuff – workplace reform, changes to legislation, government support, employer responsibility and so on. But the one thing that is going to make the biggest difference to your life once you start back at work is your relationship with your partner, and whether you organize between you a workable and fair arrangement.

Help from your partner

When our mothers, women of the generation of liberation, raised their consciousnesses and re-educated their husbands – or divorced them – and demanded the right to work *and* to fulfil themselves outside the home, they laid the red carpet of opportunity at the feet of their daughters – us. We could be whatever we chose. As women changed, we assumed that men would follow. Roles would be re-evaluated and responsibilities divided more equitably across the partnership (if we chose to have one at all).

It hasn't quite worked out that way. Women have changed, but the systems we operate in haven't kept up. We work in a man's world. The working week suits men, and the pay and promotion structures continue to work for men. And when we come home carrying a baby we usually find that we haven't won all we thought we had on the home front, either. By default or by design, blame him, or her, or blame the hormones, everything changes from that point on. Maybe it's the fact that men can't breastfeed in those early weeks and months, but somehow they get this ticket of leave from all domestic duties for the next 18 years.

Yes, they 'help'. They'll put on a load of washing 'for you', or do the shopping 'for you', or even babysit (babysit *their own children*) while you go for a night out. But somehow, suddenly, you are the owner and driver of every domestic chore and he is your 'helpful' offsider, rather than your equal partner.

Men are more actively involved in parenting now than they have been in the past. There are now stay-at-home dads and we have male politicians who read their children bedtime stories and get political mileage from knowing how to change a nappy. But these changes have been in small increments and are yet to deliver a significant shift in the who-does-what equation. The majority of men have yet to come to terms with the fact that they are an integral part of the family and are required to contribute across the whole range of emotional and domestic needs as well as economic ones.

We're getting better. Men are beginning to get it that women don't own the housework just because they have ovaries, and women are beginning to understand perhaps that 'No – that's not the way to do it. Why don't you listen?' isn't a great motivational pep talk. Not that we are all like that, but you know what I mean. We all have work to do.

Perhaps it's the way women ask for help, and we need to be more clear.

I am happy to help – in fact I am happy to do more than I do, she just has to tell me what she wants. Unless she tells me that cleaning the loo means cleaning under the rim as well or around the bottom of the bowl, or whatever, I just won't know. Men are best when they are following orders.

Andrew, two children

You can't just guess what is expected of you. How am I to know that 'have you been in the bathroom this morning?' means to her 'have you cleaned the shower, the loo, the mirror, dusted under the cupboards and put all the towels in the wash?' I just think she is asking whether I've had a shower yet. So I go off and have a shower, thinking that'll make us both happy.

Pete, three children

Or perhaps we should just let them get on with it. After all, as women, we learn our parenting skills by trial and error – but men don't often get the same leeway. We do everything ourselves because we know that we're going to get it right – from taking the crying baby away to settle, to packing the lunch boxes because *we* know what the children want in their sandwiches. And each time we do, we deny him the opportunity to learn and give him the excuse not to take on more responsibility.

> Many women become control freaks in the course of motherhood. They develop a belief that their way is the only right way. You delegate, but then you're on their case for getting it wrong. You have to let your territory go. You have to ask yourself, what's the bottom line? Is it safe? Is anyone going to get hurt? If the answer is 'no' you should just let it go. It is about getting things done. Their way is different, but difference is good. Children should experience different ways of doing things.
>
> Jacqui Marson, Counselling Psychologist

If you are used to being in charge at home, and you ask someone else to share the load, then you are going to have to hand over some of the control. It is easy to delegate tasks, but only when you delegate responsibility will you stop having to worry about every detail of everyone's lives every minute of the day and give yourself a genuine break.

The only way it works is if mothers are prepared to relinquish authority over care. You can't expect someone to assume responsibility if you don't relinquish authority. If you want a partner to do half the work, you have to let them go. If he wants to feed them baked beans every day, he can. If you are not happy you need to talk about it as equals, not giving orders.

Roni, author and publisher, three children

But, of course, it is not simply a case of asking nicely and letting them get on with it. For whatever reason – habit or genetic determination – there are times that men just don't get it:

My second day back in a new job and the pipes burst at home. Jack gets a call from the neighbours – and phones me to tell me to deal with it. I am in a new job – it's the first time I've worked for eight years – right in the middle of the induction course, and keen to make the right impression. He had no concept that I couldn't just drop what I was doing and go. He was so used to his working life being more important.

Jo, nurse, three children

I was offered a job after the Asian tsunami hit to go and set up support services in the region for an NGO. My husband was working and he said I couldn't go because he had to work, and there were three children to look after. I really wanted to go, so I thought, 'I'll see if I can take them with me'. The company which was sending me agreed and so they came. The eldest was eight, the youngest was three – and for three months the four of us shared a hotel room where we lived and I worked. It didn't occur to either Tim or me that the reason he had cited for not going in the first place – to leave him working and looking after the children – was exactly what I would be doing when I went and took them with me. When we were weeks into it, the realization came from him and he felt very guilty – but we laughed a lot that neither of us had even realized that it was the same in reverse!

Willa, three children

However good you are at this, no one gets it right all the time. It is about communication, negotiation and renegotiation. If you want to strengthen your hand and get the best possible outcome, try approaching the discussion with the clarity and the objectivity you would a business negotiation: know your goal for the negotiations; know your bottom line – what you are prepared to negotiate on and what is non-negotiable; show you are flexible by handing over some easy wins; stay calm and businesslike throughout.

Real life

It's not about one negotiation and getting it right first time. It is a series of negotiations, countless compromises and discussions – every day, and throughout the day. I offer to do the things I can do – and that I can really help with. But work commitments will come up and sometimes they have to take precedence. Plans have to change – it is a question of finding a way through it together.

Jason, producer, three children

Tips on effective negotiating with your partner

1 Negotiate when you are both calm (not in the midst of an argument).

2 Do not spring the negotiations on your partner – suggest a time when you can sit down and talk things through together.

3 Know what problem you need to resolve and if possible what help you are going to ask for.

4 Play to both your strengths. Try to divide the tasks first by what you each enjoy doing and what you are good at, then divide the rest.

5 Find out what he is prepared to offer – can you work with that, or do you need to negotiate for more help?

6 Be clear about what you *need* – not what you are angry about, disappointed by or what frustrates you.

7 Agree what is important with your partner.

8 Be specific about the nuts and bolts of who does what and delegate specific areas of responsibility. You need to know who is going to put the rubbish out, make the lunches on which days and do which school/sports/music runs.

9 Put intangibles on the list of things to negotiate too. It is easy to obsess about logistics and ignore your emotional needs as a family. This includes time to hang out as a family, individual time and time as a couple.

10 Talk about money. How is the second income going to impact on the family budget? Do you get to keep it all? Who will pay for what and how? Will it affect the family savings plan, and how much will you each keep back for yourselves?

Real life

Apart from the breastfeeding, my husband and I have had a 50 per cent split from the very beginning. Rich likes being involved. He has three grown-up children from a previous marriage and his first wife tells me they did half and half.

It is much harder for parents where the mother has been in charge and suddenly she starts working and wants the dad to do half the childcare. She has to give him half the responsibility. We've had a 50/50 arrangement ever since we got together – even before children. I had lived on my own for years and he had just got his life back after years of marriage. We bought a house that we could virtually split down the middle – it's an old farmhouse with a back staircase. We spend time together – we run a business together – but we keep separate space. The key to our success is our separateness.

Roni, author and publisher, three children

Should the one who earns the most money do the least around the house?

Just because you earn less money doesn't mean you should necessarily do more housework. When you go back to work you will need help to allow you to do the job you are employed to do – no matter if it is less well paid. If you are a nurse and he is a software developer and you both work five days a week, should you pick up his socks because he earns more than you? I don't think so. How important your job is, and how much effort you require to do it satisfactorily, is not necessarily determined by your salary.

The right combination of who does what around the house is different for everyone. But women don't *own* the housework because they have ovaries. Share it – share the work, and share the satisfaction of doing a great job and living in a pleasant environment. Or get some paid help.

Real life

We never planned for me to stay at home as the primary carer, but Jen is more career minded – she needs to be at work, so it isn't altogether unexpected. It fell to me because we returned from years living overseas and she found a job and I didn't. It has been quite an adjustment – and some people find it a bit weird – but we have a great family network, in fact grandma lives next door and Jen's sister is nearby too.

The biggest issue for me is the support networks. When Jen was at home with the baby, she was organized, and involved in playgroup, mothers' group, all sorts of things, but I find it harder to go along and get involved. The women in the mothers' group have been together from day one – they know each other so well, and I feel a bit like an outsider. I guess I should be out there being more involved, but I do find it hard to get the enthusiasm.

Jen is a great mum – and she trusts me completely. She knows that I am not sitting at home being slack. We have been together and close for a long time. We had our fights seven years ago, and they were about bigger things than housework, so somehow dealing with the domestic stuff is not a problem. I guess living in East Timor for years helped – we had a house the size of a lounge room, with no water or electricity – and we both worked from home. We learned to tolerate each other pretty well there. Mind you, when she got off the bus the other day, and I was a mess, I hadn't done anything about dinner – and we were having three people over – she went off at me, about the way I was dressed and everything else. Some of these things are not gender specific – it depends on where you are standing.

Although she enjoys her work, it is hard for Jen when she goes off in the morning – sometimes we have to boot her out the door and we try to meet her bus at the end of the day. I know she misses Sander, and finds it hard to be away from him – perhaps there is a little jealousy that I am at home all day with him.

Rik, stay-at-home dad, one child

Real life

When you have split from your partner – the children's father – the hardest thing is getting the help you need. Whatever you do, whatever you need, you don't want them to think that you need them. If I appear to need him, it is a weakness, so I always say that I am fine, that I don't need him.

Carolyn, student and part-time restaurant worker, two children

Help from your family, friends and community

How did our mothers' generation manage their working lives when few were blessed with even mildly liberated househusbands?

Usually it was to enlist the help of 'grandma', or extended family and the immediate community. Where once you could leave your child with your mother, a sister or ask a neighbour to watch out for them, for us it's not so simple. Our families are moving apart and our sense of community has changed.

We are less and less likely to remain living close to our families. If we haven't moved away from them for better job and education prospects, then our parents are moving from us as they retire – away from the cities, to the coast or increasingly to spend their retirement years in the sun. Eight per cent of UK pensions are paid abroad.

Those of us still lucky enough to live within babysitting distance of close family find things aren't quite what they used to be, either. Our mothers are busy with careers, study, hobbies and community commitments. What did we expect? They weren't going to sit around knitting booties until they got the grandchildren that we procrastinated about having for ten or even 20 years. They are getting on with their lives, down the club, up the coast, or back at work (where the government intends to keep them for as long as possible). Yes, they'll help out with the grandchildren, but we are more likely to find ourselves fitting around their busy schedule than the other way around.

Our neighbourhoods have changed too. It may 'take a village to raise a child', but we no longer live in villages. There's a lot less interaction with neighbours on the whole, and it is so easy to see ourselves as a collection of individuals living in isolation, rather than in communities for which we feel deep connection and great responsibility. Even if you know your neighbours reasonably well, would you feel comfortable about asking them to help out with the children in an emergency?

If this is your situation, it is time to create your own village: get to know your neighbours and strengthen your network of supportive friends who you can call on when you need to.

Everyone needs help from time to time, yet so many of us seem reluctant to ask for it. Just as importantly, people like to be asked to help. Being needed gives us meaning, purpose and validation. Think how delighted you feel when someone comes to you for help. You feel valued, flattered and very disposed to do what you can. Asking for help when you need it – and when it is reasonable – is not selfish. There is generosity in allowing people to be part of and to contribute to our lives.

There are thousands of women all over your town who are going through versions of what you are experiencing. They all need to talk about it just as much as you do: to celebrate their joys and triumphs, and maybe to spit and swear about the injustices of it all, as well as to ask the occasional favour. It is likely that there is at least one woman in your street who you don't know who is going through what you are, recently has done or is just about to.

Our towns can be isolating places. Find out who is around you – other mothers with children, elderly people who may be at home during the day. Knock on their doors and introduce yourselves. Let them know that you are around – and that they can call on you if they need help. Older people living around you and people new to the area will especially appreciate the effort. And you never know when you or they might need a friendly face. In our street alone this year, we have had a major blackout, burst pipes and a very damaging house fire. Knowing that there is a safe and welcoming place to take the children while you call the fire brigade is very reassuring.

Help from other support groups

Your mother and toddler group or NCT group. You have known each other for a long time, and are going through similar stages.

Work colleagues. Many will have children and other family commitments – can you help each other out from time to time?

Other parents. You will meet other parents at playgroup, crèche, pre-school and school who will not only understand the complexities of a busy schedule and offer kind words and encouragement, but can also help in more practical ways. Don't forget to offer the same support in return.

But finally, it comes to the point where you've exhausted the help you can get from partner, family and community, and you realize it's still not enough. You're going to have to bite the bullet and consider what is probably your least favourite option and, ironically, also the most expensive – paid help for childcare.

9

Childcare

Properly run and appropriately licensed childcare provides a safe, happy and stimulating environment in which to leave our children while we work. However, day care is not a substitute for being able to leave your child with family. I'm not being sentimental here, just practical. Family isn't going to turn your child away at the first sign of a runny nose or rash, blowing your work timetable and commitments. Family isn't going to fine you for every minute you are late, or leave your child at the police station if you are half an hour overdue. Day care isn't going to take your child to get new shoes when they need them or to the nurse for jabs, or hang an occasional load of washing on the line. And then there's the guilt.

Real life

I remember the first time I left Louisa with a childminder, she was only five months old. All the way there I was in a sweat – worried about whether she would be okay, whether she was too young to leave, whether she would miss me, get hungry, or if the carer would know how to settle her. I got back into the car after dropping her off and I remember this incredible and completely unexpected sense of freedom. When I drove off, I just could have driven for ever.

Alison, teacher, two children

The whole childcare issue is fraught with dos, don'ts, shoulds, shouldn'ts and who-can-afford-to-anyways? But when you are going back to work and you've got a six-month-old baby or a couple of school aged children, you don't need a debate. You need a solution, and the solution has to be high quality, affordable and local to where you live or work.

What are your options?

The range of options available to you will depend on the age of your child, what your working day looks like and what kind of hours you will need your child to be cared for, and, of course, what you determine to be the needs of your particular child. It will also depend on what is actually available within a reasonable distance of where you live or work and, finally, on what you can afford.

You need to start researching childcare as soon as you know you are going back to work. In fact, even if you are not sure whether you are going back to work or when, it is worth putting your child's name down at a childminder or day nursery, depending on your preference, as soon as you have picked it out from the baby naming book. Good childcare, especially if it is affordable, is oversubscribed almost universally. The chances of you finding the right place at short notice aren't good.

Your first task is to find out what is available in your local area. There will be government subsidized and private childcare facilities, and you will be able to get a list of these from your local authority or by calling the Childcare Link hotline on 0800 096 0296. Alternatively, you can search by postcode online at www.schoolsfinder.direct.gov.uk or parentscentre.gov.uk.

Choosing the right childcare for your child

Out of home childcare

Once you know what is available, you can go about selecting the facility that will best suit your needs and the needs of your child. The advice booklets tell you to visit two or more childminders, nurseries or day nurseries in your area, so that you can compare what is on offer and make your choice. This is good advice, but what many fail to say is that realistically your choice might be

Most common childcare options available

Childminders. For under 12s. Look after up to six children in a home setting. This can include picking up children from school and providing after-school care. Must be OFSTED registered, but need not necessarily have childcare qualifications.

Crèches. For under 8s. Provide occasional care. Usually staffed by a mix of qualified and unqualified child carers. Must be OFSTED registered.

Day nurseries. From birth to 4 or 5. Open usually from 8am until 6pm. Provide play and some early education. Usually staffed by a mix of qualified and unqualified child carers. Must be OFSTED registered.

Nursery schools. From 3 to 5. Early education during school hours only. Must be OFSTED registered.

Out-of-hours school care/kids' clubs. For 4–14 year olds. Usually run on school premises, providing out-of-hours activities and quiet time for homework. Includes breakfast clubs and after-school clubs. Must be OFSTED registered if caring for children under 8 years old.

Home child carers. Any age. Registered childminders who work in your own home rather than theirs. (Your home will need to be registered as a childcare setting if you use a home child carer.)

Nannies. Any age. Provide childcare in your own home and can look after children of any age. Usually have childcare qualifications. Not registered but can participate voluntarily in the Childcare Approval Scheme (see page 194).

Au pairs. For older children. Not qualified or registered, so not usually suitable for small babies. Will do around five hours' childcare in return for pocket money plus board and lodging. Most often young people from overseas in Britain to improve their English or on a working holiday.

limited by the length of the waiting lists, the cost of the childcare or your need to get something in place quickly in time for your return to work.

Real life

When I moved to a new area with my children aged four and three I was sent information by the council about local childcare facilities. The list looked amazing, there were lots of private and community nurseries in our area and I started to ring around straight away. I soon realized that demand for childcare meant that everything was full and there were long waiting lists for even basic playgroups. I eventually got my three year old into a nursery within walking distance, but only for three mornings a week, despite being eligible for five mornings. I learnt my lesson and if I have any more children I will put their names down for playgroup at birth.

Kate, three children

Your real choice might be more restricted than is ideal, but you should nonetheless take time to visit whatever childcare facilities are available, and to learn as much as you can about what they offer and how they work.

A good place to start is the reputation that a childcare centre or childminder has in the local community and how successful the centre is at keeping its staff. But nothing substitutes for your own inspection and evaluation and the chance it offers to meet the staff and ask as many questions as you feel you need. Taking your child along for a play will also let you know whether or not he or she finds it a comfortable and stimulating place to be. It is also worth making sure you visit while there are children around, so that you can get a picture of the 'environment in action'.

Even if the childcare facility you visit is the only real choice you have, it doesn't mean you should accept what is on offer at face value. Ask as many questions as make you feel comfortable. We are all desperate for childcare – and there is not enough to go around – but you are still a customer and have a right to understand the service you are buying.

Some questions to consider when you visit a childcare centre or childminder might be:

● Does it feel comfortable?
● Is the atmosphere warm, friendly and welcoming?

- Is the environment clean, bright and spacious?
- Do the staff look like they enjoy their work?
- Are the children happily engaged in activities?
- Do staff listen to children and answer them carefully?
- Are parents welcome to visit the centre at any time?
- Is there plenty of equipment and a range of toys in each room?
- Is there evidence of ongoing projects or interests?
- Is there an outdoor play area?
- Is information on the centre's programmes and policies readily available?
- Are parents encouraged to participate in the centre's activities and decision making?
- What kind of ongoing training do staff receive?
- What kind of food and drink is provided?
- How will you be kept informed on your child's progress and happiness?
- What is the policy on encouraging good behaviour from the children?
- What is a typical day at the centre for a child of your child's age?
- What additional services does it provide (nappy services, hot meals) – and what additional costs?
- What is the staff turnover like?
- How many children are there of your child's age?
- How are the age groups divided?

Here are some other things you may need to consider:

- Is the centre convenient to where you and/or your partner work, or live?
- Are the hours of opening compatible with your work commitments?
- What is the centre's reputation in the community?
- Are there penalties for arriving late to pick up?
- What are the fees?

In-home childcare

You may opt to have someone care for your child in your own home; the two most common options are to employ a nanny or an au pair. Nannies are expensive, and as their employer you are responsible for their payroll tax and national insurance contributions – which can add around 30 per cent to their rate. However, for some women they are the only viable option.

> **Real life**
>
> *We had our first child in a nursery for two years, but when we had our second son we got a nanny. With two children, it cost the same as the nursery, but it was more convenient, we didn't have to do the drop-off – including packing bags, spare clothes and so on – and if we are late home from work which can happen in both our jobs, there is more flexibility with the nanny than the nursery could give us. And when the children get colds or viruses, there is no issue at all. We can leave them with the nanny, and not have to take them out of the nursery and take a day off work.*
>
> Jeremy, two children

An au pair is cheaper to employ – they'll work for pocket money plus board and lodging – but they are usually not qualified, and possibly not even experienced with children, so what you can reasonably expect from them is different. Au pairs are often students who have come to the UK to improve their English or on a working holiday.

Whether you employ a nanny or an au pair, selecting someone to work with your children in your home must be done with care. Both types of help can be sourced through agencies, but ultimately the responsibility to make the right choice, and to make it work, lies with you.

Employing a nanny or an au pair

It hardly needs to be said that getting the right person is crucial if they are going to be in your home and interacting with your children. You are trusting them with everything – your children, your car, your house; they even have to get along with your pet. So how can you tell whether this person or that is going to work out?

Take recruiting your in-home childcare seriously.

First, decide what you are looking for. What kind of help do you need? What hours? What do you want the nanny/au pair to do? Think about things like preparing meals, organizing a range of activities, driving the children to school, etc., any tidying or washing of the children's things. Do you expect them to live in? Use this thinking to draw up a detailed job description.

Next, determine the terms and conditions of the job: the salary, the hours, any benefits, trial period, etc.

Your next step is to advertise the job. Both nannies and au pairs can be sourced through agencies and there are plenty listed in the *Yellow Pages*. It is also worth asking around and seeing if you can get an agency recommended to you.

Using an agency will cut out some of the work by helping you refine what you are looking for and providing a short-list of candidates. Most agencies will also ensure the applicant has a criminal records check from the Criminal Records Bureau. As an individual employer you cannot do this. Your best alternative is to ask the nanny to apply for a disclosure and show it to you. They are under no obligation to do so. Agencies will also check references – although as it is ultimately your responsibility, it is best that you check these too. Agencies will charge a fee which can be considerable for a nanny and, although less, still significant for an au pair.

An agency can also advise you on issues related to employing someone in your home – such as qualifications, pay scales, workers' compensation, employers' or public liability insurance, tax and national insurance obligations. There are specialized companies, such as Nannytax and NannyPAYE, which deal exclusively with finances related to payment and tax for nannies which will simplify these issues.

If you don't want to use an agency, you can advertise the position in magazines, your local paper, online or on noticeboards at the local library or at a college that runs childcare courses, for example. Advertising the position yourself will save you the agency fee, but it does make reference checks and work history doubly important.

In your ad, outline the hours, the ages and number of children, and the area where you live. You should ask applicants to apply initially in writing so that you can create a short-list before having interviews.

Interviewing for a nanny or an au pair

If you are interviewing an au pair from overseas you may have to conduct your interview by phone, or even email. If this is the case, it is still important to give the interview some thought, and make the most of the opportunity to find out as much as you can about the applicant – and to make sure she or he is as clear as possible about the job you are offering and the conditions of employment.

Real life

I hired an au pair from China and conducted my 'interviews' by email, although I also had a reference from a friend of her family who lived near me. As I did not want her coming all the way from Shanghai thinking it would be a holiday, I did my best to outline all the worst aspects of an au pair's job. The early mornings, the noisy bath times, the occasional toddler tantrums and the fact that childcare can sometimes be downright exhausting, as well as fun. The bleak picture I drew of life in a household with three children under five didn't put her off and her stay has been a great success. By setting her expectations at a low level before she arrived, I think she has been pleasantly surprised by the reality. I haven't felt guilty when the work becomes challenging for her, because I was honest from the beginning.

Caroline, journalist, three children

If you are employing a nanny you will certainly be able to interview face to face. Allow enough time for a thorough interview, and if possible arrange for someone to interview with you. A second opinion will be very helpful. Prepare a list of questions and take notes as you go. It will help when you come to the decision making.

Questions to consider when interviewing for a nanny should include the following:

- What training and experience do they have?
- How would they structure a day/a week with your child – what range of activities, rest periods, etc.?
- How would they provide ongoing feedback to you about your child's day and how things are going generally?
- What particular skills, interests or passions do they bring to the job – musical abilities, craft, aptitude in sports?
- Do they share your values about bringing up children – your attitude to food, discipline, watching television, exercise, hygiene, periods for play and for learning?
- Can they show themselves to be resourceful and with initiative?
- How do they interact with the children?
- Can they be flexible with their hours? If you are caught up at work or your train is delayed, will they be cheerful about staying on and providing emergency cover?
- Do you have some kind of empathy with them? (You don't have to be best buddies, but it helps if you can get along.)

Always check references from at least two previous employers. Follow up any written references with a phone call to the referee. Here are some questions to ask referees:

- Did they ever give you cause to worry about the safety of your children?
- How do they perform under stress?
- How were differences of opinion handled?
- How did they manage a dispute with the child?
- Did they do all that was asked of them?
- Did they use initiative when it was called for?
- Did they have much time off sick?
- Why did the nanny leave?

Remember to ask for proof of identity, certificates of qualifications and a disclosure from the Criminal Records Bureau (see page 194).

Once you settle on a suitable candidate, agree on the terms and conditions of the job, even if you have a casual arrangement. Things to include are:

1   A job description – what exactly you expect them to do.

2   An agreed trial period.

3   How much notice you expect for time off.

4   The amount of annual leave they will be given and how much of it is paid.

5   Arrangements for sick pay.

6   Arrangements for public holidays.

7   Arrangements for paying tax and national insurance.

8   Whether they are covered by employer and public liability insurance – you can get this from your house insurers.

If you can work from home for a few days when you are introducing a new childcare arrangement, you will get a sense of how the carer gets on with the children and how he or she disciplines them and manages any problems, calms them down and so on. It will be a great reassurance to you. But mind you stay out of the way. If you hover too obviously, neither the child nor the carer will get a chance to settle into the new arrangement.

Once you find someone you and the children trust and like and it is working well, do what you can to keep them. Replacing a reliable nanny, au pair or babysitter isn't just a question of finding someone to do their hours. You and your children have to build a whole new relationship and it can take weeks until things are running smoothly again. Agree regular times that you will sit down with the nanny and discuss how things are going – so any problems are recognized early and dealt with as they emerge.

Quality controls

All registered child carers and childcare environments – private or government run – for children from birth to eight years old are subject to a range of controls such as the number of children cared for, the ratio of carers to children, what training and qualifications carers must have, criminal records checks and health and safety standards that must be observed. They are inspected and registered by OFSTED in England, the Care Commission in Scotland, the Northern Ireland Social Care Council in Northern Ireland and CISW in Wales. Inspection includes health, safety and educational standards, as well as a criminal records check for all the carers.

You can ask to view a childminder's or a centre's Certificate of Registration, or look at the OFSTED report for the centre online at www.ofsted.gov.uk.

A further level of quality assurance is provided by the Investors in Children quality assurance scheme, which encourages child carers to join up to programmes which offer ongoing mentoring and advice about improving their service, in return for quality assurance endorsement. To find out whether childcare services in your area are involved in such schemes, you can search at www.surestart.gov.uk.

The Childcare Approval Scheme is a new government-backed initiative to introduce some quality assurance to unregulated child carers, such as nannies working in private homes. The idea is that your nanny voluntarily registers with an approving organization which imposes certain criteria, such as the requirement of a up-to-date first aid certificate, before issuing approval. If your nanny participates in this scheme then you will be eligible to claim the childcare element of the Working Tax Credit and Employer Supported Childcare Tax and NICs exemptions (see page 194 for financial support available for childcare). You can get further information by phoning the national helpline on 0845 767 8111 or visiting the website at www.childcareapprovalscheme.co.uk.

Real life

The whole process of registering our nanny with a childcare approval scheme has taken months – and it's costing money. It is a great idea in principle and the tax relief would be very welcome, but so far there has been a fee to apply, a fee for the Criminal Records Bureau, a fee for a course in first aid, and we have dealt with about five different bodies – the police, the approving agency, the people who ran the first aid course, our local authority which issues the childcare vouchers, my payroll department, even a special department at my employer called the work and family balance team. And we still haven't finished the process. To be honest, trying to pull the whole thing together has probably cost me more in time than we are going to save in tax through the scheme.

Jeremy, doctor, two children

Useful resources when you are looking for childcare

Finding childcare

www.childcarelink.gov.uk or call 0800 096 02 96 – for details of your local Childhood Information Service (CIS). The CISs provide face to face or phone advice on all aspects of childcare. Can download the useful leaflet 'Choosing Childcare – what to look for. The top ten questions to ask' from the site.

www.surestart.gov.uk – for information on location of childcare centres and quality assurance programmes for child carers in England. Can download its 80-page booklet, 'Looking for childcare'. You can also order the booklet by calling 0845 60 222 60. The Sure Start website also has a useful section on how to go about selecting and employing a nanny.

www.dfes.gov.uk – the Department for Education and Skills publishes a free information booklet, 'Making childcare choices 0–7', which can be downloaded from its website.

Quality assurance and regulation

www.ofsted.gov.uk – for reports on all registered childcare facilities.

www.crb.gov.uk or the Criminal Records Bureau Information line on 0870 9090 811 – for information on criminal records checks.

www.childcareapprovalscheme.co.uk or call 0845 767 8111 – for information on the Childcare Approval Scheme.

Financial assistance with childcare

www.hmrc.gov.uk/childcare; www.inlandrevenue.gov.uk and the Tax Credit Hotline 0845 300 3900 – for information on tax credits and the effect that employer provided childcare vouchers might have.

What financial support is available to help with the cost of childcare?

There is government support to help with the cost of childcare. It comes in the form of:

- **Working Tax Credits.** Working Tax Credits are not restricted to working parents, but there is a childcare element for people with children, up to 1 September after the child's sixteenth birthday or up to the age of 19 if they are in full time, non-advanced education. Lone parents can claim the childcare element for registered or approved childcare if they work 16 hours a week or more. Couples can claim it if both work at least 16 hours a week, or one partner works at least 16 hours a week and the other is incapacitated, in hospital or in prison. The childcare element can help with 80 per cent of eligible costs up to £175 for the costs of one child, £300 for the costs of two or more children.

- **Childcare vouchers.** These are provided by your employer in return for salary sacrifice. The first £50 a week of these is not subject to national insurance contributions or tax. May affect your entitlement to Working Tax Credits – so check the benefit (online or with an accountant).

Details of what you are entitled to and how to claim the benefits can be found at www.hmrc.gov.uk/childcare or www.inlandrevenue.gov.uk/taxcredits, or by calling the Tax Credit Hotline on 0845 300 3900 (in Northern Ireland, call 0845 603 2000).

This is the practical side of the childcare issue. But what about the children? How do they cope with being dropped at nursery as we head off to work? Is there anything we should do to prepare them – or indeed ourselves? Chapter 10 provides some thoughts on the children's role in all of this.

A word about the children

So how do the children fit into all this?

It's funny. Women can fly planes, run governments, take the business world by storm. They can make films, design incredible buildings, lead space missions, swim with sharks if they have to. But the hardest thing for so many women, no matter what they do in their working lives, is to walk away from home, nursery, childminder, grandparent or stay-at-home dad with the cries of their baby ringing in their ears: 'Mummeeeeeeeee, don't go!'

You'd think that we'd invented work just to torture them.

You know the scene: the white-knuckled, red-faced toddler clinging desperately on to the nursery gate screaming as if it is about to be abandoned; the distraught mother leaving the scene shaken and teary eyed. You'd have to be a plank of wood not to respond – not to question your commitment to work and wonder about the wisdom of your choices. Not only do you have your child's pleading eyes (and ear-piercing scream) but you also have the latest research from childcare gurus and early development experts splashed across the headlines: 'Children do better with mummy', 'Nurseries are bleak and frightening – a nightmare of bewildered loneliness'.

Let's get a few things into perspective.

First, the little bit of drama that kicks off your toddler's day may wreck yours, but nine times out of ten he or she will be happily absorbed in play dough, the whole incident wiped from memory, before the cries stop ringing in your ears.

Second, it is not about whether you work – it is about you leaving. When a toddler gets it into his or her head that you have to be there 24/7, it's non-negotiable – you'll get a version of the same scene whether you are off to work, off to the supermarket or shutting the door for a private moment on the loo. Don't confuse your baby's developmental stage with a social debate on the rights and wrongs of two-parent working families.

Third, whether you stay at home all the time, work ten hours a week or 50, your child will want you there more than you are. Being the centre of the universe is part of being a child – realizing that they're not is part of growing up.

And finally, put the 'experts' into perspective. There is only one expert in you, your child and your choices, and that is you. Why, when we find it so hard to take advice from our mothers, are we so susceptible to the words of men and women who have never met us and don't even know the name of our child, just because they come to us through the media? Remember, bad news sells better than good, and books that tell us what we're doing wrong are always going to outdo ones that congratulate us on getting it right. This is especially the case when the subject is parenting, and the audience is made up of anxious, guilt-susceptible women and men who just want to do the best they can, but discover every day just how hard that can be.

So what do you do? Do you start back to work as early as you can, so that your child hasn't had time to form a bond with you? That would have to make the separation easier! Or do you give up work despite yourself (and your bank balance) until your child is old enough to do without you (aged about 40) and you can return to your career guilt-free?

It is time for the debate to move on from whether or not women should work, and what damage it is or isn't doing their children. If the childcare that is available to working parents is not up to scratch, shouldn't we be putting our intellectual and financial resources into changing that? We are not going to stop women working, after all. Women have always worked – whether they carried their children into the fields on their backs, or left them with their mothers when they went into the factories.

The debate on whether or not women should work has had its day. We also need to leave behind us the debate on whether it is *mothers* who are failing their children when two parents have a career. Children whose mothers work are not automatically deprived of parental care – children do have fathers and fathers are more and more involved in the nuts and bolts of bringing up their children. And where they are not, they need to be. Attitudes to flexible work arrangements for both parents and social attitudes to stay-at-home dads need to be supportive and encourage fathers – and shift the debate away from whether mothers are or aren't doing the right thing.

I'd like to know which early childhood expert got to my four year old, whose ideas on working parents are quite clear:

Daddy works because he has to, to earn money to buy us a house and everything. Mummy only works because she wants to.

Chloe, 4

Do children suffer because their mothers work?

The model of parental working is worldwide, and it's traditional. There is no evidence to show that children suffer as a consequence. On the contrary, parents who are happy, purposeful and have financial security are better positioned to help their children grow into contented and confident adults. Work is very much part of this picture.

Of course, there is evidence to show that a lack of appropriate care can affect a child's development. But do we sometimes confuse the heart-wrenching images of babies in underfunded, squalid orphanages in desperately poor or war-affected regions of the world with the average OFSTED-registered day nursery in our local area? If childcare facilities are not up to the standard that they should be, our society is wealthy enough to put that right – and educated enough to make it a priority.

All children need to be in an environment that meets their emotional, developmental and physical needs. But it doesn't have to be with their parents, not all the time. Children benefit from a variety of influences and models of behaviour – not the whims and the whiles of only one adult carer for better or for worse. Children, especially young children, are so much more adaptable than we are and so much more accepting of change than we give them credit for.

Give yourself a break after all! Your parenting to this point hasn't been so weak that your child is going to fall apart the moment you turn your attention away from them, has it? You have been a careful and thoughtful mother, laying the foundations that allow your children to grow into confident and independent beings. Of course, they'll notice a difference when you head out of the door at an unusual hour, and return with your head full of issues and pressures that have very little to do with their sleep patterns, school work or sports fixtures. But as long as they feel safe, are appropriately supervised and know where their next meal is coming from, children will adapt to most things.

And surely a working mother, with the right childcare to support her, can provide a well-balanced, well-rounded upbringing for her child, in today's world.

Preparing older children for your return to work

As children get older, and can talk about how they feel, you can discuss your work commitments with them and what they will mean in practical terms to the whole family. It is worth taking time to understand their perspective on the new arrangement, both at the beginning and as it works itself out over time. You are likely to find that they are coping better than you think – and can be thoughtful and creative about ways they like to make up for lost time with you, when they do get you to themselves.

Start by filling them in on what is going on and why. Give them a chance to let you know how they feel about it, then include them in planning how the family is going to adjust. Give them some real responsibility and make them feel part of the team – not part of the problem that needs to be resolved in order for you to get on with your life. And help them to see what they are going to get out of it.

Here are some tips on preparing your children:

- Talk to them about the change that is going to happen.
- Explain why you are going back to work and what you and they will get out of it.

Real life

Basically you are not around, and they want to know why not. They understand that it means we are going to get more money. So they want to know how they are going to benefit – what they are going to get out of it. With my children, I told them to write down a list of things they wanted, or they wanted to do, and agreed that over a period of time they would get some of these things. They are in before- and after-school care. I had to let them see there was something in it for them.

Carolyn, two children

- Explain to them how it will affect their day to day lives – when you will be around, when you are likely to be unavailable and who will look after them. Timetables and calendars that mark out routines as well as things to look forward to, like special dates and holidays, can help children feel things will soon be predictable and 'normal'.

- Allow them choices where practical. Will they go to after-school care or to a friend's house? Will they do a sports camp during the school holidays or go and stay with grandparents?

- Ask them to think of what they can do to help. Even very young children thrive on responsibility and being made to feel part of the team. Write up a list of chores and put it on the fridge.

- Work out what rewards the children will get for helping out. Limit offers of presents and other material compensation – it is not a substitute for time with you, which is what they really prize.

Manage your moods and your stress, whether or not you work

Children don't suffer because their parents work, but they may well be affected by their parents' stress. If you find that you are bringing home the stresses of your working day and taking it out on your children – either directly or simply because you find you are not always the bouncy, happy-go-lucky, I'll-just-toss-these-nuggets-in-the-oven-and-my-children-will-blossom-and-my-husband-will-love-me woman in the ads – then you might want to consider how you manage your stress.

But once again the question you ask yourself shouldn't be, 'I'm stressed, and the children are suffering, is my working damaging the children?' but, 'What can I do to better manage my stress?' After all, work isn't the only source of stress in our lives. Families, relationships, finances, how we view ourselves can all be sources of stress – some of which are alleviated by earning money and improving self-esteem, both of which are associated with being out at work.

How you manage your stress has a lot to do with how well you look after yourself. Missing meals, drinking too much and going to bed late are not stress management techniques. They sap your stamina and are likely to make you *more* tired and grumpy – trust me, I've tried them. (See Chapter 11 for some advice on staying fit, healthy and sane while running around after the children and keeping your career on track.)

When stress does explode all over the children, take time to reassure them that it is not their fault – then move on. Avoid loading yourself down with guilt, and if you think it is part of a pattern, see what you can do to relax better – or get help.

Forget the chores and focus on the children

The good news – and the bad news – is that what children want most from their parents is *time*. It's good news because it can save you a fortune in expensive trinkets you may be tempted to buy to make up for your absence. It's bad news because the one thing working mothers don't have is time. And when we do get a bit of time with the children it is usually at those mad rush times of the day: bundling everyone out of the house in the morning – nappy bag, clean clothes, shoes, lunches, sports gear, work clothes, laptop, etc.; or 'arsenic hour' at the end of the day – tired and hungry adults, rushing to pick up tired and hungry children, driving them home, tea, bath, reading, homework – and then finally, bed.

It is worth thinking about though. It is so easy to focus on the chores we have to do to keep our lives ticking over, and to forget the relationships that make our lives worthwhile. Finding some chore-free time to be with your children – at their own pace and on their terms – is important to them.

Young people want their parents – not exclusively their mothers – around for special school events, celebrations, sporting achievements and when they are having problems. They also want 'hang time' – time just to be in their parents' company, hanging out with them with no strings attached.

Real life

I mostly don't mind that Mum and Dad both work. But when I get home at six o'clock, if I have been in after-school care, then I like to spend time with them relaxing, not go out or anything, just have a normal evening, eat dinner, watch telly, read together – they read to me or I read to them – or take the dog for a walk with my dad. It's good to have ways of relaxing together at the end of the day.

If we all get home at six o'clock and I haven't seen them all day, and they haven't seen me, I am really pleased to see them, and I really enjoy their company – and they enjoy my company too.

If they have to work extra hours, they usually make it up to me by trying to have a normal day at home. If I was given the choice of a present or money or something or spending some time with Mum or Dad to make up for their working extra-long hours, I would probably take the time with them.

Alistair, 11

Investing in time with your children will pay off. In terms of contributing to their development into happy, healthy adults, it beats ironing their clothes, home-baked cakes and dusted skirting boards (apparently some people still do this). Just to make sure, I have also stopped hoovering, picking up any clothes off the floor and cleaning out the fridge.

If you can find a few moments to sit down with them, among the mess if need be, to listen to their stories, laugh at their jokes and tackle the occasional 'if people die and are buried, how long

What is 'quality time'?

Spending frequent small amounts of time with children can be more beneficial than less frequent longer periods of time. [...] Time that is special to your child will occur when your child approaches *you* to tell you something, ask a question or involve you in their activity. When this happens, and you are not occupied with something important, stop what you are doing and make yourself available. If you are busy at the time, try to plan some time for your child as soon as you can.

From the Positive Parenting Program – Triple P

before they grow back?' kind of question, you'll be doing all right. If for a few moments you can block everything else out and concentrate exclusively on them, it can sustain you both for the day.

How often you should do this depends on which study you read – so the best answer has got to be 'as often as you can'. It probably won't be as often as you'd like, it almost certainly won't be as often as your children would like. But if it is as often as you can (and as honestly as you can), if it is not clouded by guilt, regret or remorse, and if you can both come away smiling – you are being a great mum, and you are doing a fabulous job balancing your work, your life and your family.

Finally, a word about you

Which of these have you done in the last week?

- Eaten lunch
- Exercised for 30 minutes
- Laughed out loud
- Spent some time on your favourite hobby – yes, you can definitely include shopping
- Met up with an old friend
- Been to the cinema, *without* children
- Congratulated yourself on how wonderful your children are turning out to be
- Slept undisturbed for eight hours
- Done some yoga/meditation/stared into space while someone rubbed your feet
- Accepted a compliment with a smile and a thank you
- Had a long hot bath on your own
- Had a long hot bath with a friend

Before you are a working mother – or a mother-who-works – you are a person. You are a *woman* for goodness sake – and women have needs. Women need to be cherished, nurtured, nourished, rested, entertained, indulged and pampered – in ways that no one else ever quite understands. And because no one else ever quite understands, it is perfectly legitimate to nurture, nourish and indulge ourselves from time to time. In fact, when you are the centre of the complex operation of running a family and holding down a job, it is your moral responsibility and a medical necessity.

If you can honestly answer 'yes' to at least four of the items from the list above every day, then I guess you are in pretty good mental shape. Many of us will be doing well to aim for four of the items a week and there'll be some weeks when you achieve none.

Physical stamina and a good mental attitude are the absolute cornerstones of everything you are setting yourself to achieve as a working mother. Remember (as if you'd forget), you want to be the best mother you can and get the most out of your working life, but you want to have some fun too – and you have to make sure that you do.

Without wishing to sound alarmist, becoming a mother is fraught with plenty of its own mental traps. There is no need for us to add to them by not taking care of ourselves. The incidence of post-natal depression, estimated to affect between one in six and one in ten new mothers, is not evidence that so many of us are flaky and not up to the job. It is a testimony to how intrinsically difficult the adjustment to motherhood can be:

The transition to motherhood is such a monumental life change that 90 per cent of women struggle with it. It is painted as only a happy event, but in reality it is associated with a series of losses. It is normal to have problems adjusting. Who can live up to the media image of happy, perfect mummies? A huge number of mothers end up thinking that they are failures. Massive adjustment is intrinsic to the experience.

Jacqui Marson, clinical psychologist

Good health is about a decent diet, regular exercise and plenty of sleep. It is also about good mental health – a positive attitude, commitment to the choices you make, belief in your abilities and creating a supportive and understanding environment for yourself. It is about giving yourself permission to take a break, accept a compliment and have the occasional massage.

As you work out your own version of the work/family balancing act, it is important to have confidence in your ability to make the right decisions for yourself and your family. Not everyone will agree with every decision you make. That is not important. But it is essential that *you* believe in what you are doing and what you are trying to achieve. It is normal to feel self-doubt, guilt and fear and to have family rows, but they sap energy and detract from what you are trying to create. To stay sane, believe in yourself and surround yourself with people who support the choices you make. If you can get them to help with the babysitting as well, all the better.

Staying sane

The first key to staying sane when you go back to work is to acknowledge that a little bit of insanity is normal – feeling slightly out of control at times, a bit out of your depth and that you aren't quite coping as well as that woman in the cornflakes ad. There will be days when nothing seems to come together, just like there were before you had children. On the other hand, there will be times when everything goes so well you'll think you are ready to teach a juggling master-class. Hang on to those times!

The second key has to be about being honest – honest about how you are feeling, honest about what help you need, honest about what is frustrating you and bloody honest about how well you are doing.

If you can keep your expectations of yourself realistic, and stay honest with yourself, it is just a question of organizing the help you need and managing the logistics:

1 **Prioritize.** You are not going to be able to do it all, so work out what is really important to you and let some of the other things slide, or subcontract them out if you can afford to.

2 **Don't give up your support systems.** Whatever it was that kept you sane before you coupled up, had children and went back to work is now more important than ever. Whether it was netball, dancing, Turkish baths, long walks – keep them going. Think of them as preventative medicine.

3 **Be flexible.** As you know, learning to be a parent is learning that you can't control everything. Plans and priorities are always changing. Trying to lock down all possibilities and all variables is impossible and will just increase your stress.

Plan, of course, but accept that your plans will have to change sometimes.

4   **Accept that you can't please everyone all of the time.** No matter how hard we try, sometimes we have to let someone down today in order to carry on tomorrow. Do it judiciously and with a sense of your priorities. And don't feel guilty about it afterwards!

5   **Get enough sleep.** Most adults need eight hours' sleep a night. It is so tempting when you have struggled through the day's 120 chores to steal time for yourself late at night. That is all right from time to time, but you can live longer without water than you can without sleep. Make sure your general sleep patterns are healthy.

6   **Use your support networks.** Ask for help when you need it. Make sure there is someone you can call on when things are difficult.

7   **Have some fun.** There is a lot out there to be had – don't forget to join in.

8   **If you are concerned about depression, seek help.** Try your doctor. Airing your worries will help. Don't worry about being a moaning mummy – depression and anxiety are very real and can be extremely debilitating, and they can be effectively treated with support, medication and therapy. If you are uncomfortable about talking to your doctor or don't think that you are being offered the kind of help you need, talk to friends or colleagues about how to find a counsellor. It is now estimated that as many as one in ten women experience post-natal depression. There is more empathy and understanding out there than we sometimes imagine.

A few words about guilt

Most of us know what maternal guilt feels like. Whether it is snapping at your children when you are tired, having a c-section rather than a natural birth, or ignoring their musical genius and blowing their chances to star in the latest TV talent quest, there is plenty of scope for parental guilt. Going back to work – after

Real life

I had post-natal depression after both my children were born. The first time it happened I didn't know where to get help. When I went to my GP she was really concerned and wanted to help, but she kept telling me to wait another week or two just in case it was sleep deprivation that was making me feel so terrible. I didn't want to ring MIND or anything – I didn't feel it was an emergency – but after six weeks I rang a friend who had had a baby a few months before me. I told her how I wasn't sleeping even when the baby was snoring his head off and about how panicky I was feeling. She came over straight away and got me in to see a psychiatrist who specialized in PND. I am so glad I talked about it otherwise I might never have got help.

Amanda, librarian, two children

weeks, months or years – can be yet another opportunity to fuel the engine of guilt, if you let it.

But before you heap it on to the cart of emotional baggage that you drag around with you, remember that guilt has to be one of the least useful emotions. It doesn't *do* anything, it doesn't solve anything. Feeling guilty doesn't make your children happier or better adjusted. It doesn't get your house clean or help you pay the bills. In fact, guilt weighs you down, drains your energy and stops you moving on.

If there are things that you feel bad about and can fix, concentrate on them. But you can't fix everything, so if something is beyond your control, learn from it if you can, then move on.

Guilt busters – reasons not to feel guilty

1 According to a US study, children in two-parent households are getting ten hours a week more parent time (four with dad, six with mum) than they were in 1981, despite the fact that the number of working mothers has risen by 25 per cent.

2 For every working mother who feels guilty about the lack of time she spends with her children, there is an at-home

Real life

...guilty that my job cuts into my time with the children; guilty I don't walk them to school; guilty that I don't do their homework with them every night; guilty that they don't learn French; guilty that we don't visit old people; guilty that my children don't have big trees, a stream and more open space to play; guilty that the creek is now polluted; guilty that Louis doesn't learn music; guilty that I don't paint with them more; guilty that they eat too much chocolate; guilty that I don't do reading with their class; guilty that they don't shower every single night; guilty that I'm cranky; guilty that the political world sucks and I don't have time or am too selfish to be activist [and instil this in the children]; guilty that my husband and I don't go away sometimes; guilty that I don't see my girlfriends/old friends; guilty that my house and my children are messy...

Felicity, art director, two children

Real life

I know you are supposed to be wracked with guilt as a working mother but I just can't find it in me. I know my children get such good care when they are not with me. And they are happy, confident children. I can't see that having two working parents has done them any harm. I think it is good for them to know that all grown-ups are the same, and to be looked after by different adults with different personalities and tolerances.

Roni, three children

mother feeling guilty about the lack of *quality* time she spends with her children.

3 For every working mother who feels guilty about missing their child's first steps, first words, first tantrums, there is an at-home mother feeling guilty about the experiences she can't provide for the children and the things she can't buy for them.

4 Childcare can be beneficial. A recent, long-term study of 14,000 children and their parents in the UK showed that the

only difference in the emotional development of children in childcare and at home at four weeks, six months, 24 months and three years was in the six month olds. They were more likely to be fretful and difficult for at-home mothers than for working mothers.

5 Your going back to work may help promote a good relationship between your children and their father. In families where both parents work, fathers are more likely to be involved with the children and at a younger age.

6 Your children won't think you are a bad mother because you work. A US study looked at how eight to 18 year olds viewed their parents' parenting skills, evaluated against a series of 12 measures linked to healthy development, readiness for school and success at school. Working parents performed no worse than non-working parents.

7 Guilt can be very expensive. Parents often try to buy their way out of their guilty feelings. A recent Australian study showed children were happier with an explanation and some special time with their parents to make up for occasions when one has had to work extra hours or travel.

8 Guilt is negative. It doesn't fix things. It doesn't change things – and it can be contagious. Don't pass it on to your children!

9 Your feelings of guilt about how you are bringing up your children are probably more to do with your own early experiences than how good a mother you actually are. Gaining an understanding of these early experiences will give you some context for your feelings and perhaps put them into perspective.

Staying healthy

It's a tired old cliché – look after yourself and you will be in a better state to look after everyone else. And in a tired, old clichéd kind of way, don't we always know it's good advice and promise we will get more sleep, more exercise and eat better – when we get a bit of time?

The decision to take care of yourself is yours. No self-help guru, advice from a best friend or kindly word from your partner that you are putting on a bit extra around the hips is going to motivate you. A couple of pages of the same from this book aren't going to convince you either. But that won't stop me from trying.

Being healthy will not only make you more resistant to illness, it will also increase your stamina and give you a great mental boost. It is important to stay fit – for your own well-being as much as for your family.

Exercise

> Most mothers, especially working mothers, are more tired from the low levels of fitness than from a busy lifestyle.
>
> Sharon Donaldson, parent craft nurse

Going back to work is a great opportunity to get more active. You are more likely to get incidental exercise if you catch public transport regularly and need to walk to the bus stop or station. You get regular meal breaks at work, and the excuse to go out and grab a sandwich can give you the break you need from your desk, fresh air, exercise and a meal – luxuries that many women at home forget to indulge in reliably.

Being back at work will make you more aware of your fitness levels and how you stack up to your pre-maternity-leave body. It is easy to ignore the fact that you are putting on extra weight when you are at home, in loose fitting, child friendly, casual clothes. But your average office friendly outfits will let you know if you are having to hold your stomach in more than you would like to.

Ways to exercise without laying out for Lycra

Walking

- Try to walk to do your errands. You don't need any expensive gear, and if your child is in a pram then they can come with you. Set yourself a decent pace. Covering one kilometre in 15 minutes is a good speed; another test is exerting yourself enough that you can still talk, but not sing.

- When you go to a restaurant, park two kilometres away and walk. (Not for a night out in stilettos, of course.)
- Get off the bus one or two stops earlier than you need to.
- Stop driving the dog to the park for its walk.
- Meet friends for a walk, not a coffee.
- If you want to be more adventurous, find out about the Walking for Health initiative walks in your area at www.whi.org.uk.

▶ ## Some useful tips on staying active include:

1 Think of movement as an opportunity, not as an inconvenience.

2 Be active every day in as many ways as you can.

3 Put together at least 30 minutes of moderate-intensity physical activity on most days, if not all.

4 If you can, also enjoy some regular vigorous activity for extra fitness and health.

(Courtesy of *The National Physical Activity Guidelines for Australians*, issued by the Department of Health and Ageing, Australia)

Swimming

Have a swim and a sauna at your local pool before going out for a meal. When you get to the pub or restaurant afterwards you will be more relaxed and less tempted to dump the day's baggage on your loved one the minute you sit down. (You might fall asleep halfway through the meal, though.)

Cycling

Cycling is a great way to exercise. The National Cycle Network offers miles of cycle routes on quiet lanes and traffic-free routes, all detailed on its website at www.sustrans.org.uk. Key in your postcode to find local routes. The London Cycle Network offers a similar facility for cycling in London at www.londoncyclenetwork.org.

Ask yourself:

- Can you cycle to work? Or cycle with the children to school?
- Why not organize a picnic with friends – and everyone cycle there?

Doing chores

Hoovering the house for 30 minutes can be a good workout. Recommend it to your husband.

Playing with the children

- Dance with the children (or without if they laugh at you).
- Join in throwing the ball, climbing trees, racing around the park, playing in the pool.

Get an exercise partner

Exercising with someone will help motivate you and make the exercise a social event.

Join an organized event

Sign up for a fun run. It doesn't have to be the London Marathon – although that certainly would get you fit. Your local council or sports centre may have details of sports events. Or contact your favourite charity. Fun runs and other physical challenges are a common way to raise money. Get involved and you'll have the double benefit of feeling healthier and doing something for a worthy cause.

Eating well

Going back to work may well help you to improve your diet. At least on the days you work, you will have a lunch break – which may be short and you may choose to take at your desk, but it is an opportunity to make sure you stop and eat a meal.

Unless you are going to be working from home, going back to work also gets you away from the fridge – and the 'I don't have time to make myself a proper meal, so I'll just snack from the fridge 50 times during the day' syndrome. (This is closely related to the 'I don't need lunch, I'll just finish the children's leftovers – it'll save on the washing up' syndrome.) Both are bad habits – you are better off without them.

Eat a healthy, balanced diet. Avoid fad weight-loss programmes. They don't last, set you up for failure and can damage your health. Eat breakfast every day. Eat lunch every day. Drink lots of water. A handful of vitamin supplements and a latte do not make a nutritious meal.

The experts advise us to eat less sugar, butter and margarine; eat moderate amounts of milk, cheese, yoghurt, lean meat, fish, legumes, poultry, nuts and eggs; and eat mostly cereals, bread, fruit and vegetables. (They don't mention muffins, cappuccinos or leftover birthday cake – so presumably these are at your discretion.)

Sleep

Ah, the magic word! There is only one rule for sleep – get as much of it as you possibly can. Adults need an average of eight hours' sleep a night. When was the last time you got that regularly, uninterrupted? Lack of sleep – or constantly disrupted sleep – can cause fatigue. Fatigue impairs your judgement, shortens your attention span and can make you accident prone and forgetful. It reduces your motivation and makes you less efficient. Sound familiar?

If your children are in sleep patterns that involve waking you in the night – coming into your bed, or getting you up to find their rabbit and tuck them back in – you might want to sort them out before you go back to work. Your health visitor or local child health clinic will have advice and will be able to put you on to sleep professionals and behavioural psychologists if you need more specialist help. Don't be afraid to ask. Getting proper sleep can turn your life around – and you are going to need it more than ever once you are back at work.